LORD,

HOW IS IT

DONE?

LORD,
HOW IS IT
DONE?

FIVE PRINCIPLES FOR ACTIVATING
CHRIST'S ATONEMENT IN YOUR LIFE

KEN GIBSON

Covenant Communications, Inc.

Cover image: *The Prayer of Enos* © Jorge Cocco Santángelo. www.jorgecocco.com

Cover design copyright © 2020 by Covenant Communications, Inc.

Published by Covenant Communications, Inc.
American Fork, Utah

Printed in the United States of America
First Printing: August 2020

26 25 24 23 22 21 20   10 9 8 7 6 5 4 3 2 1

ISBN 978-1-52441-313-2

THIS BOOK IS DEDICATED TO MY CHILDREN
AND GRANDCHILDREN, WHO I PRAY WILL
SEEK AND MAINTAIN A *HOPE IN CHRIST*.
(SEE MORONI 9:25)

TABLE OF CONTENTS

INTRODUCTION

Learn of me, and listen to my words; walk in the meekness of my Spirit, and you shall have peace in me. (D&C 19:23)

ALL OF US WILL EXPERIENCE something in our lives that will make us long to have that promise fulfilled in a very personal way. An event or circumstance will overwhelm our ordinary powers of reason and determination and leave us feeling helpless or despairing. Too often, these experiences test our faith, weaken our hope, and make us spiritually vulnerable.

Many of the challenges we face are the ordinary day-to-day travails of mortality to which we are all subject. But others can be heavier and more enduring. Some last a lifetime. Any can feel insurmountable and can test our capacity to cope if we are not spiritually prepared. Often, our challenges bring us to our knees. Regardless of their origin or scale, the common denominator of these experiences is that they rob us of peace.

When these periods occur, it can feel like the Savior is very distant. Sometimes, this sense of spiritual isolation leads us to conclude that Christ is no longer mindful of us or that we have somehow become unworthy of His help and attention. If we allow that thought to take root, we may find our faith in Christ waning and crumbling at the very moment we need it to give us strength and sustenance.

If this describes your present condition, you will likely find the message of this book meaningful. It presents five principles that will help increase your hope and faith in the Savior and in His ability and desire to comfort, heal, strengthen, and enable you to conquer the challenges you face. These principles will expand your understanding of atoning grace and help you access its power. Yes, this book certainly invites you to come unto Christ.

But it doesn't stop there. Its purpose is to teach you *how* to come unto Him and obtain the peace His Atonement offers (see Moroni 10:32 and Enos 1:7).

A SIMPLE QUESTION

The title of this book is drawn from a well-known scriptural account: the story of Enos, a man whose spiritual crisis led him to have a day-long "wrestle" before the Lord while hunting beasts in the forest. Here is how he described his struggle and what it prompted him to do:

> And *my soul hungered*; and I kneeled down before my Maker, and I cried unto him in mighty prayer and supplication for mine own soul; and all the day long did I cry unto him; yea, and when the night came I did still raise my voice high that it reached the heavens. (Enos 1:4, emphasis added)

Perhaps you too know what it feels like to have your soul "hunger." That may even be the reason you picked up this book! If so, you may find the Lord's response to Enos particularly hopeful:

> And there came a voice unto me, saying: Enos, thy sins are forgiven thee, and thou shalt be blessed. And *I, Enos, knew that God could not lie*; wherefore, *my guilt was swept away.* (Enos 1:5–6, emphases added)

The sudden outpouring of peace he received prompted this response from Enos: "Lord, *how is it done?*" (Enos 1:7, emphasis added).

That question gives us insight into Enos's utter surprise at what he had just experienced. In essence, he was saying, "Lord, please explain this to me. Why do I suddenly feel resolved when just moments ago I was wrought up and wrestling?" He was trying to make sense of the light and comfort that had so unexpectedly come to him.

So, what *did* happen to Enos?

Yes, he received an answer to his prayer and obtained a remission of his sins, a blessing we should all desire and seek. But beyond that, Enos gained an even deeper insight. He discovered for himself that Christ's Atonement was real. He learned that it was powerful enough to fill a hungry soul, because it had just filled his. He knew there was no other way to explain the sudden change he felt in his spiritual condition.

From the moment Enos's "guilt was swept away," the Atonement of Christ was no longer simply an unexplainable concept or mysterious idea to him. He learned in an intimate way what atoning grace feels like. He found out for himself that the Savior's invitation and promise—"Learn of me, and listen to my words; walk in the meekness of my Spirit, and you shall have peace in me" (D&C 19:23)—is true. And he learned that truth the only way it can be learned—by experiencing it.

We all need to feel the healing power of the Savior's Atonement when our souls hunger, do we not? And like Enos, we cannot fully understand how it is done until we too experience it. Because God is "no respecter of persons" (Acts 10:34; see also verse 35), we can be assured that the Savior's grace will be extended to us, just as it was to Enos, if we will follow the path that grants us that access.

So what is that path, and how do we find it? What steps should we be taking to fill *our* hungry souls? How do we obtain an experience with atoning grace as Enos did?

I believe the answers to those questions are found in the five principles we will discuss in this book. Through their application, the despair, worry, temptation, and sorrow we confront in mortality can be replaced by abiding peace, joy, and confidence. These principles empower us to become spiritually self-sufficient, enable us to more clearly recognize the Savior's tender mercies and outstretched hand when we are in the middle of our own wrestles, and transform our afflictions into learning that can be consecrated for our gain (see 2 Nephi 2:1–2). They lead to an abiding *experience* with Christ's Atonement.

Two Certainties

The five principles we will discuss are rooted in two eternal truths:

1. Our ability to overcome the adversity we face on Earth is completely dependent on the mercy and grace Christ freely offers. Were it not for His Atonement, we would be powerless to overcome hardship and difficulty (see Mosiah 3:17).
2. A true understanding of the meaning and power of atoning grace can be obtained only by experiencing it, and that experience comes by

demonstrating faith and hope in Jesus Christ through our attitudes and behavior. It cannot be acquired through study alone.

Accepting these truths is essential to our spiritual progress. But that is where most of us get stuck. We do not know how to turn our *belief* in those truths into *actions* that grant us access to the Savior's grace. And so, we find ourselves asking the same question Enos did: "Lord, how is it done?" The difference is we want the answer to that question at the *start* of our trials, not just at their resolution.

Truth be told, it is not completely our fault that we struggle with this issue. We grapple with it partly because we are taught *who* performed the Atonement, *why* it was necessary, and *what* purpose it serves, but we are not always taught *how* to go about laying claim on its power right now, to help us with the difficulty we are facing *today*. As a result, the Atonement can sometimes feel to us like an incomprehensible and unapproachable idea rather than the means of personal support and solace it is intended to be.

This lack of understanding has led to an unfortunate phenomenon in the Church. Many faithful members believe in Jesus Christ and have a testimony of His Atonement, yet their suffering is unrelieved. By that I mean they experience some measure of emotional or spiritual pain that the Savior is willing and able to remedy, but *they* are unable or unwilling to surrender. In effect, they do not *allow* Christ to heal them. I believe this occurs because they simply do not know how to lay claim on this promise:

> Come unto me, all ye that labour and are heavy laden, and I will give you rest.
> Take my yoke upon you, and learn of me; for I am meek and lowly in heart: and ye shall find rest unto your souls.
> For my yoke is easy, and my burden is light. (Matthew 11:28–30)

This phenomenon can be dangerous because unaddressed burdens incur a spiritual and emotional cost that compounds over time. When our pain is magnified and extended rather than relieved and resolved, we can end up pursuing solutions that lead us away from the true Source of relief and healing instead of drawing us closer to Him. As that separation broadens, we lose hope and begin to question what we really believe. These are high costs indeed.

We can know we are exhibiting symptoms of this phenomenon if we find ourselves describing our feelings and circumstances in terms such as these:

- *I have overwhelming feelings of grief and sorrow* about the possibility of losing my spouse, who has been diagnosed with a terminal disease. There is a *constant pain in my heart.*
- *I feel great anger and bitterness* toward my former spouse in the wake of our divorce.
- *I feel powerless* to help a wayward child and *am grief-stricken* by his choices and how they are affecting my family.
- *I feel incomplete and discouraged* because I have not yet married.
- *I am frustrated* that I am not overcoming my impatience and quick temper, and *I feel unworthy* as a result.
- *I am guilt-ridden* over serious sins I have committed and *feel completely lost and desperate.*
- *I have feelings of abandonment and anger* because God has not answered my prayers by allowing me to bear children.

We say these kinds of things when the difficulties we face seem insurmountable. And we feel this way because we have allowed ourselves to think we are on our own to overcome such trials and afflictions. As a result, we end up relying solely on our limited mortal capacities to address our challenges. Because that idea *is* so overwhelming, we give in to feelings of discouragement, worry, and despair and allow them to guide our decisions and actions.

The reality is we cannot do it alone. More importantly, we don't have to! Through Christ, we can receive strength not only to endure the trials we face but to emerge from them with greater spiritual capacity than we had before they began (see 2 Nephi 2:1–2). This is the miracle of His Atonement.

As a result, the title question of this book—*Lord, How Is It Done?*—is relevant to each of us as we confront the challenges mortality imposes. How do we transform our belief in Christ into an experience with His Atonement? How do we move from despair to hope, then on to faith, peace, comfort, and healing? How do we lay claim on atoning grace to "make weak things become strong unto [us]" (Ether 12:27)?

These are the issues I seek to resolve in *Lord, How Is It Done?* The book begins by asking you to embrace hope as a real power that will help you face challenges and adversity in a productive way. It ends with an invitation to more fully claim the privileges and fruits of atoning grace. That fruit has been described as "precious" and "sweet above all that is sweet" (Alma 32:42; see also verse 41). As you move through each chapter of this book, you will learn "line upon line, precept upon precept" (2 Nephi 28:30) how to experience Christ's Atonement in a real and abiding way by challenging yourself to put the five principles to the test. By applying the principles taught here, you can have your own Enos-like experience—one relevant to *your* circumstances and the things with which *you* wrestle.

Indeed, the Savior's Atonement is the only solution to the seemingly unresolvable issues, injustices, and (perceived) disparities in our lives. There are no boundaries to the problems it can solve or the pain it can remedy. And although it is *infinite* in its reach, it is also *intimate* in its influence. Christ's ministrations are personal, not general. His gifts are tailored to each of us based on our circumstances. We simply need to learn how to more frequently and effectively call upon those gifts to work their miracle in our behalf.

The Savior's grace is a manifestation of His infinite love for us, born of the sacrifice He made in our behalf. Of His grace and love, President Dieter F. Uchtdorf taught:

> He extends many gifts and His grace to us every day. He promises to be with us, to come to us when we need comfort, to lift us when we stumble, to carry us if needed, to mourn and rejoice with us. Every day He offers to take us by the hand and help transform ordinary life into extraordinary spiritual experiences. (Dieter F. Uchtdorf, "Of Curtains, Contentment, and Christmas," First Presidency Christmas Devotional, 2011.)

My hope is that this book will help you lay claim on the blessings President Uchtdorf describes. My intent is to show you how it is done so you too can "transform ordinary life into extraordinary spiritual experiences."

Special Note: The principles discussed in this work came into clear focus for me while I was serving as a bishop in Southern California. In that capacity, I served with individuals and families who were at various stages of their own Enos-like wrestles. In this book, I share some of their accounts, each with permission. In some instances, the name of the individual spoken of has been changed to preserve his or her confidentiality.

ENVISION THE POSSIBILITIES

AS THE SPIRIT CHILDREN OF a Heavenly Father, we are high growth-potential beings. Among other things, this means each of us is an unrepeatable miracle possessed of unique gifts, qualities, and purposes. In fact, we came to Earth with an inherent capacity to become like God (see D&C 76:58, 84:38).

Because of our divine heritage and destiny, our Father provided a Savior to empower us to overcome our limitations and achieve our eternal potential. In addition, He has given us the means of learning the truth of who we really are and Christ's role in helping us become like Him. He has endowed us with agency— the power to decide whether we will adopt a hope-inspired view of our mortal experience or a view steeped in pessimism and victimization. God gives us the freedom to pursue joy and spiritual prosperity or surrender to despair, worry, and sin. Here is how Lehi explained it:

> Wherefore, men are free according to the flesh; and all things are given them which are expedient unto man. And they are free to choose liberty and eternal life, through the great Mediator of all men, or to choose captivity and death, according to the captivity and power of the devil; for he seeketh that all men might be miserable like unto himself. (2 Nephi 2:27)

Despite all the reasons we have to approach life with faith-fueled optimism, some reject hope as a realistic option for addressing their present circumstances. Perhaps they either see hope as a naive notion or just do not know how to use it as an engine of spiritual progress.

With that in mind, the aim of this opening section is to teach about the Savior's power to invigorate hope and provide an escape route to overcome those things that weigh us down or cause us despair. This section teaches why His Atonement is the only power that can help us navigate the challenges and pitfalls mortality imposes.

Hope requires us to consider the possibility that things can improve, that we will weather the storm and emerge stronger tomorrow than we are today because of how we dealt with a difficult experience. It invites us to consider what can be and not just what once was or what we once did. It asks us to live our lives out of our imaginations, not just our memories.

We can do that only if we have a means of addressing or letting go of unfulfilled hopes, past misjudgments, and unexpected events in life that paralyze us. The means whereby we obtain hope is called grace and is available because of the power and reach of Christ's Atonement. Grace enables us to use the principle of hope as a change agent and grants us the ability to take action toward a new and better way of thinking and living.

With that in mind, let's examine how to envision the possibilities.

CHAPTER 1
Choose Hope

Hope is an emotion which brings richness to our everyday lives. It is defined as 'the feeling that . . . events will turn out for the best.' When we exercise hope, we 'look forward . . . with desire and reasonable confidence' (dictionary.reference.com/browse/hope). As such, hope brings a certain calming influence to our lives as we confidently look forward to future events. (Steven E. Snow, "Hope," Ensign, May 2011.)

> KEY UNDERSTANDING 1
> The first step toward experiencing Christ's Atonement during challenging times is to choose to be hopeful rather than pessimistic and despairing (see Moroni 7:41).

Daily Life

In 1995, Janet Lee (wife of former BYU President Rex Lee) shared a story in the *Ensign* that I think effectively frames the core challenge of mortality:

> When our daughter Stephanie was five years old, I took her to register for kindergarten. When we arrived, she was invited to go into a classroom to participate in some games with the teachers and other children. As a former elementary school teacher, I knew the games were designed as tests for placement purposes.
>
> A teacher was sitting just outside the room with a box of crayons and several sheets of blank paper, and I smiled confidently as Stephanie was asked to choose her favorite color and write her name. *She can write all the names in our*

family, I thought. *She is so well prepared, there isn't anything in that room she can't handle!* But Stephanie just stood there. The teacher repeated the instructions, and again my daughter stood still, staring blankly at the box of crayons, with her knees locked and hands behind her back.

In the sweet, patient voice that teachers use when they are beginning to feel slightly impatient, the teacher asked once more, "Stephanie, choose your favorite color, dear, and write your name on this paper." I was about to come to my daughter's aid when the teacher kindly said, "That's okay. We will help you learn to write your name when you come to school in the fall." With all the restraint I could gather, I watched Stephanie move into the classroom with a teacher who believed my daughter did not know how to write her name.

On the way home, I tried to ask as nonchalantly as possible why she had not written her name. "I couldn't," she replied. "The teacher said to choose my favorite color, and there wasn't a pink crayon in the box!"

I have reflected on this incident many times over the years as I watch my children grow and as I observe life in general. How many times are we, as Heavenly Father's children, immobilized because the choice we had in mind for ourselves just isn't available to us, at least not at the time we want it?

Is progress halted when acceptance into a chosen field of study is denied, when a desired job doesn't materialize, when marriage or children are unfulfilled dreams, when health limitations present unforeseen obstacles, or when money hoped for isn't there? Are we ever, for reasons that are hard to understand or beyond our control, faced with a set of circumstances that we did not have in mind for ourselves? In other words, what happens when we look in the box, and the pink crayon just isn't there? It is so easy to lock our knees, put our hands behind our back, and do nothing when things wished for and dreamed about are beyond our reach. But to do so would defy the very reason we are placed here on this earth. As hard as it sometimes is to understand, stumbling blocks are essential to our progression.

(Janet Lee Chamberlain, "Choices and Challenges," *Ensign*, February 1995. Used by permission.)

Principles

Sister Lee's story about crayons is a perfect metaphor for our mortal experience. Life is seldom all we want or expect it to be. And because it sometimes disappoints, it is easy for us to be paralyzed by our circumstances. When that occurs, we *desire* our life to be better but find it hard to envision how that is possible. So we feel stuck.

Heavenly Father's plan for our exaltation includes a probationary period during which our ability to remain true and faithful will be tested. And when we look into the metaphorical crayon box and find our favorite color is not there, we can know we are experiencing such a test. However, our Father did not leave us to fend for ourselves during these periods of struggle. The Atonement of Jesus Christ was planned and carried out precisely because the Savior knew mortality needed to include periods of opposition (see 2 Nephi 2:11). Because we have a Savior, we can approach life with confidence, knowing joy is within reach even if we are not fully experiencing it right now (see 2 Nephi 2:25; Matthew 11:28–30).

However, simply knowing this truth does not fully help us. We need to be able to transform our *desire to believe* a better future is possible into a *fulfillment of our hope and faith* (see Alma 32:21, 27; Hebrews 11:1; Ether 12:19). So how do we do that?

To move beyond our struggles and get to a better place in our lives, we must first envision what *better* looks and feels like. Certainly, none of us will be motivated to make changes in our perspective or behavior unless we are compelled by a superior picture of life to the one we are currently experiencing. Why would we be? If we cannot foresee a future that is better than the present, there is little reason to change—or to think that our efforts can lead to anything higher, richer, or more exalted. And unless we have *defined* the ideal to which we aspire, it is impossible to pursue it.

In contrast, once we fix our minds on a specific and inviting image of what we want our lives to be—with hope-filled anticipation—the path leading to it begins to manifest itself almost magically. That is the miracle of hope. Our spirits *intuitively* move toward the improved life picture we have envisioned, because we each possess a divine guidance system called the Light of Christ (see D&C 84:46–48). As we act in faith by deepening our commitment to patterns of righteousness, that light grows brighter, and the Savior endows us with the power to overcome the things that are constraining us. That power is called grace, and it compels us to keep going, quite literally yoking us to the Savior (see 3 Nephi 27:15; Matthew 11:28–30; Bible Dictionary, "Grace"; Principle Five). This is what hope means and how it works.

An Exercise in Hope

Understanding, then, the implications of the missing crayon phenomenon Sister Lee described, let's talk about how we can acquire greater hope. If we want to become more confident about our future, we must change our perspective and improve our vision of what is possible. And to accomplish this, most of us need a plan: something concrete we can do or follow that will help us envision a better condition and start moving toward it.

Personally, I have found a five-step process valuable for addressing challenges that are holding me captive or otherwise keeping me from experiencing joy and fullness. I believe this process can transform the spiritual and emotional barriers we often experience into opportunities that increase our faith. As I explain the steps in the exercise that follows, consider how each step applies to your present circumstance and how it can help you adopt a more hopeful approach to dealing with adversity. And since increasing hope is the aim, you may find it useful to write down your responses to the questions posed in each of the following steps:

1. **Your Present Condition.** How would you describe the struggle you are currently facing *and the feelings it has created*? (Review some of the expressions of despair included in the Introduction of this book for examples of how you might frame those feelings.)
2. **Where You Want to Be.** In what ways would your life be better if that issue were resolved, and how would you feel? (This might include statements such as: inner peace will replace feelings of anger or bitterness, I will experience more self-control, I will gain spiritual confidence, or I will have a clear conscience.) Think about this long enough to get a vivid picture firmly fixed in your mind; then commit to reviewing it frequently.
3. **Things That Could Stop or Deter You.** What potential barriers or obstacles could keep you from achieving the better future you have

just envisioned? (This might include things such as associating with the wrong people, entertaining negative or self-defeating thoughts, or neglecting righteous habits.)

4. **Potential Solutions.** What are some ways you can overcome those barriers or things you can do to keep those obstacles from having any real impact? (Here, you may consider the following: make covenants and commitments with Heavenly Father, increase time spent studying the scriptures, or spend time with uplifting people.)

5. **Strengths and Experiences.** What are some of the strengths you possess and past experiences you have had that give you confidence your life can and will get better? (In this part, you might include the following: having a testimony of prayer, having the ability to exercise self-discipline, or receiving a patriarchal blessing.)

After completing this process, I encourage you to organize your thoughts into something I call a *Hope Roadmap*. This provides a way to capture your thinking more completely and gives you something to reference when your optimism wanes. Each person's roadmap will be unique, but following is an example of the kinds of things it might include.

HOPE ROADMAP

VISION STATEMENT

A year from now, I am free from the burden of bitterness that I have been experiencing. As I wake up each day, I am able to ponder, pray, read the scriptures, and I feel enriched by the experience. My heart is full of gratitude for my blessings and for the understanding I have of truth.

WHY I SHOULD FEEL CONFIDENT

I have capacity for patience in other areas of my life, so I know I can exercise it here also.

I have experience with prayer and know my prayers have been answered many times.

I have a desire to have my life filled with compassion, kindness, peace, and goodness.

POTENTIAL BARRIERS

I sometimes have a rebellious attitude.

I have a tendency toward selfishness and self-pity.

I sometimes try to control others rather than focusing on myself.

I am sometimes casual in my church attendance.

I sometimes partake of the sacrament without full purpose of heart.

WAYS TO OVERCOME BARRIERS

I can increase my obedience.

I can seek opportunities to serve.

I can focus only on things over which I have control.

I can commit to being at all my Sunday meetings.

I can prepare in advance for the Sabbath.

I suggest making it a habit to review your roadmap at least once a month. Weekly would be better. This will help keep you rooted in hope and provide a concrete course of action you can take to increase your faith and strengthen your spiritual resolve.

As you continue to revisit these steps and refine your roadmap, I encourage you to reject any negative thoughts that might dissuade you from believing an envisioning exercise like this can help you overcome your difficulties. The principle of hope suggests that it can and will.

THE ABSENT REDEEMER

Working through this process typically reveals a gap between where we are now and where we want to be. Without a means of bridging that gap, feelings of hopelessness can overwhelm our spiritual progress and keep us from the peace, joy, and rest the Savior has promised (see John 14:27). And while the steps we have just covered are important, they are not enough to effect the transformation we need if we want to experience abiding spiritual confidence and peace.

A sustained state of unhappiness or despair is evidence that a critical healing influence has been rejected or is otherwise missing in our lives (see Alma 41:11). I refer to this missing force as *The Absent Redeemer* because it represents a power that *could* help us but is not doing so, because we haven't yet learned how to access it. When that power remains untapped, we pay a spiritual price that compounds over time. That price can be manifest in a variety of forms, such as lost or impaired relationships, unfulfilled potential, wasted time, missed opportunities, a broken spirit, and feelings of bitterness and guilt. If not remedied, those costs will compound and could ultimately lead to the loss of eternal life.

Conversely, if we can learn how to turn *The Absent Redeemer* into *The Present Redeemer*, we will gain the power to bridge the gap between despair and peace. When we cross that bridge, we will find greater spiritual strength and increased peace. This newfound positive momentum will also manifest itself in different ways, such as full and meaningful relationships, a life of purpose and contribution, feelings of spiritual security and confidence, peace of mind and conscience, and a reputation of integrity and respect.

Graphically, we might depict the contrast just described as follows:

PEACE

"I feel a sense of peace, joy, and confidence and that I have the power to fulfill my spiritual destiny."

REWARD: Full and meaningful relationships, a life of purpose and contribution, feelings of spiritual security and confidence, peace of mind and conscience, a reputation of integrity and respect.

THE ABSENT REDEEMER: THE INABILITY TO RECOGNIZE AND GAIN ACCESS TO THE RESCUING AND STRENGTHENING POWER CHRIST MAKES AVAILABLE

DESPAIR

"I feel trapped, burdened, and hopeless and that there is only darkness on the path ahead."

COST: Impaired relationships, unfulfilled potential, wasted time, missed opportunities, a broken spirit, feelings of bitterness or guilt.

The force that bridges the gap between these two extremes is the strengthening and healing power that is available because of the Atonement of Jesus Christ. That power is called grace (see Principle Five). In a way incomprehensible to us in our mortal state, Christ's act in the Garden of Gethsemane and on the cross of Calvary unleashed a redeeming and rescuing gift that makes it possible for us to clear every barrier and fill every void in our lives. By drawing upon that gift, our condition and frame of mind can change, and the gulf between darkness and light can be bridged. Far too often, Christ is *The Absent Redeemer* to us because we insist on carrying our burdens alone. But because of grace, we do not have to.

This new, more enlightened perspective might be illustrated as follows:

PEACE

"I feel a sense of peace, joy, and confidence and that I have the power to fulfill my spiritual destiny."

REWARD: Full and meaningful relationships, a life of purpose and contribution, feelings of confidence, peace of mind and conscience, a reputation of integrity and respect.

THE PRESENT REDEEMER: LAYING CLAIM ON THE PEACE, STRENGTH, AND COMFORT OFFERED THROUGH THE ATONING GRACE OF JESUS CHRIST

DESPAIR

"I feel trapped, burdened, and hopeless and that there is only darkness on the path ahead."

COST: Impaired relationships, unfulfilled potential, wasted time, missed opportunities, a broken spirit, feelings of bitterness or guilt.

Christ descended below all things (see D&C 122:8–9) so He could rescue us from the depths of our trials and carry us to a more hopeful and spiritually secure place. His Atonement is a comprehensive gift. It is a gift of liberation. It is a gift of compassion. It is a gift of enablement. It is a gift of empowerment. It is a gift of peace. It is a gift of love. (See D&C 88:33.)

Our Savior wants us to be filled with hope and faith. His promise is that because of His Atonement, we can change, improve, overcome, and progress day by day. When we fall, His grace grants us the strength to pick ourselves up. His sacrifice was made to enable our success and endow us with the power to achieve exaltation. His desire and power to help us did not die with

Him on the cross but rose with Him in the Resurrection. As a result, He wants us to treat Him as a *present*, not an *absent*, Redeemer.

CHAPTER 2

Rely on Truth

Few—very few—are entirely bereft of at least one solace-giving memory: a childhood prayer answered, a testimony borne long ago, a fleeting moment of perfect peace. Our present, of course, is shaped by our past. We are in many ways its product. But at the same time, we tend to reinterpret the past on the basis of the present. We are creatures of the moment, so, rather than remember, we reconstruct what once we knew in the light of present uncertainty or loss, which can all too easily overwhelm what we once held as true and real. All too often we forget the gentle impressions we felt, the calm soothing of troubled hearts and minds, or even greater manifestations of divine love. (Terryl Givens and Fiona Givens, The Crucible of Doubt: Reflections on the Quest for Faith, *[Salt Lake City, Utah: Deseret Book, 2014], 116–117. Used by permission.)*

KEY UNDERSTANDING 2
To increase our hope in times of adversity, we should review and remember the assurances of truth we have experienced in the past.

Daily Life

One winter, I took my twin grandsons skiing at Deer Valley, Utah. They were eleven years old at the time, and none of us had ever been to the resort before. It was a stormy day and snowed most of the time we were there.

After we had taken a few runs in the lower part of the mountain, we decided to explore the lifts and trails higher up in the resort. In the course of that exploration, we landed on the top peak of Deer Valley at 9,600 feet. As we ascended to that high point on the mountain, the storm grew more intense, and the wind started blowing harder.

When we got off the lift, we made our way toward the run we planned to take for our descent. However, as we moved in that direction, the wind and snow were so furious we could barely see a few feet in front us. So we worked our way slowly and carefully toward what we hoped was the right route. Being unfamiliar with the trail we were following, we moved with some trepidation.

Because the wind and snow were blowing so hard, I failed to observe that one of my grandsons had become quite upset and fearful. Finally, I heard him cry out, "Grandpa, I'm scared!"

I assured him everything was okay and that if we just kept moving in the direction we were headed, the run would lead us down to the less-stormy part of the mountain, where we had been before taking the lift to the top. "We just need to keep going," I encouraged him. "We can't go back up, and we can't just stand still." I did not, however, let on that I too was fearful and felt a bit uncertain about how best to deal with what we were facing. I knew my grandson trusted me to lead us to safety, so I did not want to say anything that would lessen his confidence or add to his concern.

Ultimately, as hoped and anticipated, we made our way to the calmer area of the resort below and resumed a great afternoon of skiing. Needless to say, we did not return to the top of the mountain that day.

The following morning, the twins and I were in the kitchen having breakfast. "Guys, I'd like to talk about what happened at the top of the mountain yesterday," I began. "I know it was a bit scary, and I want you to think about how you would handle a situation like that if you were alone and not with me. Let's discuss how you should think and what you should do."

I proceeded to explain that whenever we face a challenging situation, instead of panicking, we should focus first on the things we already know or have experienced that can help us figure out the best way to solve the problem. In other words, we should draw from the frame of reference our past represents to guide us in our present circumstance. I explained, "Yesterday we were caught in a blinding snowstorm at an unfamiliar ski resort. So let's think about things you know from past experiences that could help you if you ever find yourself in that situation by yourself. For example, although you had never skied at Deer Valley before yesterday, you have skied at other resorts. You have been on dozens of ski trails, so you know, based on your experience, that if you just stay within the boundaries of the run you are on, it will lead you to the bottom of the hill." Continuing, I added, "Your experiences skiing elsewhere also tell you that sooner or later, other people will be going on that run. They will pass by, and you can ask them for help. In most cases, those people will have been on the run before and can give you guidance based on *their* experiences."

I gave them several other examples of things they knew or had previously been through that could provide guidance if they ever again found themselves skiing in a snowstorm. I concluded with this: "And, of course, you can *always* pray. You can ask your Heavenly Father for help, then listen for the promptings of the Holy Ghost. If you act on the things He tells you to do, you will be okay."

Principles

At some point, everyone faces intense spiritual, emotional, or physical challenges. When difficulties like this arrive, most of us feel unprepared to deal with them, much as my grandsons and I did when we encountered the unexpected storm at the top of Deer Valley. These tests can weaken our spiritual resolve and make us vulnerable to the influence of the adversary. Satan wants us to choose despair over hope and inaction over faith. Consequently, when he sees we are even a little off-balance, instead of extending a helping hand, he pushes us. He *wants* us to lose our footing and fall. He has no interest in seeing us remain upright and stable. And once we hit the ground, he plants his foot firmly on us and does everything he can to ensure we cannot get up (see D&C 10:5–6, 12, 20–28).

Because that is true, when periods of unexpected adversity arrive, the most productive response we can have is to reflect on the truths we know and the experiences we have had that give us confidence that we can navigate the current storm we are facing (see Alma 32:27–34). Why? Because those reflections stabilize us and keep us from falling. They protect us against Satan's designs. These remembrances and learnings can calm our fears and guide us in our decision-making.

As Terryl and Fiona Givens indicate in the quote that starts this chapter, few of us go through life devoid of experiences with the Lord's tender mercies. Perhaps we have felt comfort or reassurance from the Holy Ghost, received a blessing from heaven that was both obvious and meaningful, or had an unexplainable feeling of confidence when all logic said we should feel otherwise. These experiences have been given to us, at least in part, so we can draw upon them when life serves up its storms.

This is likely what the Lord had in mind when he counseled Oliver Cowdery in one of *his* moments of confusion and concern. As you read the instruction Oliver received, substitute your name for his, and imagine the Lord is speaking directly to you. See if the things Oliver was told are also relevant to your circumstance.

Behold, thou art Oliver, and I have spoken unto thee because of thy desires; therefore treasure up these words in thy heart. Be faithful and diligent in keeping the commandments of God, and I will encircle thee in the arms of my love.

Behold, I am Jesus Christ, the Son of God. I am the same that came unto mine own, and mine own received me not. I am the light which shineth in darkness, and the darkness comprehendeth it not.

Verily, verily, I say unto you, if you desire a further witness, cast your mind upon the night that you cried unto me in your heart, that you might know concerning the truth of these things.

Did I not speak peace to your mind concerning the matter? What greater witness can you have than from God?

And now, behold, you have received a witness; for if I have told you things which no man knoweth have you not received a witness? (D&C 6:20–24)

The reservoir of experience from which we can draw as we navigate challenges is unique to each of us. Although we may share some things in common with others, no two people have lived the same life or bring the same frame of reference to their present circumstance. However, what *is* the same is our need for the guidance and reassurance eternal truths can offer during turbulent times.

Despite our individual differences, truth remains constant and is revealed equally to all who seek it (see Acts 10:34–35). Revealed truth teaches that we all have the same spiritual heritage, that we are on Earth for the same purposes, and that the requirements for salvation and exaltation are identical for everyone. Most importantly, this truth teaches that we all depend equally and completely on the Savior to overcome our trials and become like our Father.

Consequently, as we look to past experiences to inform the approach we will take to our present situation, we should go one step further. We should use our challenges as an opportunity to deepen our understanding of principles and doctrines that are intended to guide our actions during mortality. This blending of experience and truth turns hope into a viable solution when we are in despair.

With that in mind, let's review three truths that should inform our perspective in everything we do but especially during times of adversity.

THREE TRUTHS

The scriptures define truth as a knowledge of things as they are, as they were, and as they are to come (see D&C 93:24). That definition is a key to maintaining our spiritual equilibrium throughout mortality. Accepting that definition should lead us to ask a couple of questions anytime trials arrive: "How should the truths of where I came from, why I am here on Earth, and where I am headed after this life influence how I deal with my *present* circumstance? And what experiences have I had with those truths that give me confidence that I can successfully address the challenge I currently face?"

In the Book of Abraham, we learn three doctrines about our eternal identity that are relevant to every mortal experience we encounter—good or bad:

1. We are literal sons and daughters of a Heavenly Father, who is God. We lived with Him before coming to Earth, and our destiny is to become like Him and inherit all that He has. He loves us with an infinite love and is motivated by pure intent in everything He does.
2. Mortality is part of our ascension toward exaltation. It is just one segment of our celestial evolution—the second of three *estates* we will experience on the path to our eternal destiny. It is a testing period in which we exercise our agency in order to develop a godlike character.
3. Christ's Atonement connects who we were in our premortal existence with what we can become in the eternity that lies ahead. His sacrifice makes it possible for us to discover and *re*cover our eternal identity so we can realize our celestial potential.

These three truths offer us an enlightened view of mortality and what our experiences here are meant to teach us. When we are tempted to shrink in the face of adversity, we should look at our circumstances in the context of these three doctrines and see what conclusions they help us draw. Like confronting the storm my grandsons and I encountered at the top of the ski resort, such remembrances can save us from despair and lead us to a calmer place. So let's examine these in more detail.

Truth 1: *We are sons and daughters of God.*

> Thus I, Abraham, talked with the Lord, face to face, as one man talketh with another; and he told me of the works which his hands had made;
>
> And he said unto me: *My son, my son* (and his hand was stretched out), behold I will show you all these . . . and I saw those things which his hands had made, which were many; and they multiplied before mine eyes, and I could not see the end thereof. (Abraham 3:11–12, emphasis added)

God referred to Abraham as His son. He did the same with Moses and many others whose accounts we find in the scriptures. Through prophets, God has referred to you and me the same way. Here are just two examples:

> "I have said, Ye are gods; and *all of you are children of the most High.*" (Psalm 82:6, emphasis added)

> "Beloved, *now are we the sons of God,* and it doth not yet appear what we shall be: but we know that, when he shall appear, we shall be like him; for we shall see him as he is." (1 John 3:2, emphasis added)

Brigham Young explained the nature of our eternal identity this way:

> There is no spirit but what was pure and holy when it came here from the celestial world . . . They were not produced by any being less than our Father in heaven. He is the Father of our spirits; and if we could know, understand, and do His will, every soul would be prepared to return back into His presence. And when they get there, they would see that they had formerly lived there for ages, that they had previously been acquainted with every nook and corner, with the palaces, walks, and gardens; and they would embrace their Father, and He would embrace them and say, "My son, my daughter, I have you again;" and the child would say, "O my Father, my Father, I am here again." (Brigham Young, *Journal of Discourses,* 4:268. Used by permission.)

Imagine the impact it would have if we acted in accordance with this truth whenever we faced a mortal challenge or temptation. We are the offspring of God, who taught and trained us in a premortal existence called the first estate (see Abraham 3:26). Our lives on Earth are both temporary and necessary in our growth toward an eternal inheritance (see D&C 84:38). Our Father loves us, wants to help us, and has provided atoning grace through His Only Begotten Son, Jesus Christ, to strengthen and enable us. These truths should reassure us that however bad our circumstances might be, they are both temporary and preparatory. They are leading us toward something more exalted.

Truth 2: *Mortality is an essential step in our ascension to exaltation.*

> We will go down, for there is space there, and we will take of these materials, and we will make an earth whereon these may dwell;
> And we will prove them herewith, to see if they will do all things whatsoever the Lord their God shall command them. (Abraham 3:24–25)

This explanation of why our Father sent us to Earth provides context for everything that happens to us here. The second estate is not a sentence or punishment imposed upon us because of the Fall of Adam and Eve. Rather, the actions of our first parents created the opportunity for us to have a mortal experience in which we could apply the eternal truths we learned while in the presence of our Father. The second estate is an essential part of the plan. Therefore, the time we spend in mortality should be viewed as an important step in our ascension toward exaltation—one that enables us to become what we are divinely endowed to be *if* we use our agency properly. This truth prompted the Lord to instruct Joseph Smith (and the rest of us) that he should view all things he was asked to endure as "experience [that would be] for [his] good" (D&C 122:7; see also 2 Nephi 2:1–3).

In mortality, God wants us to discover our divine nature and allow it to become the ruling force in our lives. This is why He has given us His gospel. In it we find His law, and living the law unveils our *true* nature. This is because the law embodies and reveals *God's* nature (see Dallin H. Oaks, "Love and Law," *Ensign*, November 2009). Therefore, by obeying the law, we gain a more complete understanding of who we really are, how the truth of our divine identity is relevant to the struggles we face, and what our focus should be in this second estate (see John 17:3; Moroni 7:48).

Because we cannot see the future and do not remember our premortal past, we need revelation from our Father to know how best to address our present circumstance. Therefore, faith and trust become essential ingredients for dealing with adversity. They allow revelation to flow more freely through the spiritual channel revelation relies upon (see 1 Corinthians 2:9–13). Increased faith comes from increased obedience to the law. As faith, trust, and obedience work together, our spiritual vision is expanded and the purpose of our struggles becomes more apparent.

This enlarged understanding of our eternal nature and of the purpose mortality serves in our celestial development should change our perspective about the trials and tests we face. It should lead us to ask, "How does the Lord want me to respond to this challenge? What does He want me to learn? What is He trying to teach me through this experience?"

Truth 3: *A Savior was provided.*

> And the Lord said: Whom shall I send? And one answered like unto the Son of Man: Here am I, send me. (Abraham 3:27)

This exchange between Christ and our Father is only meaningful if we accept the first two truths of our eternal identity we just discussed. The Savior's mission was necessary because the divine characteristics our Father helped us nurture and develop prior to sending us to Earth are hidden from our view here. In mortality, we are subject to temptation and often succumb to the lesser parts of our nature (see 1 Corinthians 2:14; Mosiah 3:19). It takes time for our spirits to gain control over our physical and emotional desires and appetites. Before we mature spiritually, those terrestrial tendencies tend to rule over us. This state would continue if we were not offered a power that could help us overcome our baser inclinations and achieve self-mastery.

This spiritual vulnerability would hold us hostage if a redeeming force were not made available to rescue us. The conversation between the Father and the Son as recorded in the Book of Abraham teaches us that the Savior said *He* would perform that rescuing mission; he would condescend to make it possible for our eternal character, reflexes, and instincts to be uncovered, renewed, and made enduring in mortality (see 1 Nephi 11:16–22, 31). He did so because He knew our fallen state would make it impossible for us to accomplish that cleansing and renewing process on our own. We would need a compensating and reconciling power beyond our self-will.

So One who understood perfectly the eternal worth of our souls volunteered to become our Savior and Redeemer. He was sent to provide the means of revealing and restoring to each of us our true identity so we could grow in His grace until the perfect day (see D&C 18:10–11; 50:24–25; 88:15–18, 21; 93:11–13). It is the renewing and refining power of Christ's Atonement that gives each of us the ability to reconnect with our eternal or spiritual self—line upon line and precept upon precept (see D&C 98:12). The Savior bridged the gap this second estate creates between our premortal selves and the people we will become when we obtain our exaltation. He enabled each of our eternal identities to be revealed and restored and to remain.

These three truths should grant us a more hope-filled view of our present circumstances. Because we have knowledge of both our divine heritage and celestial inheritance and have been given the means of overcoming all things in mortality through the saving power of Christ's Atonement, we can truly "look to God and live" (Alma 37:47), knowing it is going to be okay. C. S. Lewis said it this way:

> [Mortals] say of some temporal suffering, "No future bliss can make up for it," not knowing that Heaven, once attained, will work backwards and turn even that agony into a glory. . . . The Blessed will say, "We have never lived anywhere except in Heaven." (C. S. Lewis, *The Great Divorce*, 69.)

Either in this life or in the next, all will be made right, and all will be well.

CHAPTER 3

Trust the Savior

The changes, and resulting challenges, that we encounter in mortality come in a variety of shapes and sizes and impact each of us in unique ways . . . Although each 'change' may be unique to our individual circumstances, there is a common element in the resulting trial or challenge—hope and peace are always available through the atoning sacrifice of Jesus Christ. The Atonement of Jesus Christ provides the ultimate corrective and healing measures to every wounded body, damaged spirit, and broken heart.

(W. Christopher Waddell, "Turn to the Lord," Ensign, November 2017.)

KEY UNDERSTANDING 3
Our power to rise above our challenges and lay claim on an experience with atoning grace relies upon our ability to trust the Savior.

Daily Life

Bishops spend a certain amount of their time working with people who are either considering divorce or have already terminated their marriages. The divorce experience usually leaves those involved spiritually and emotionally wounded. Most of the people I met with in this circumstance wrestled with significant disillusionment, anger, and confusion. Many questioned, "I did what I was supposed to do, so why did this happen to me?" Their confidence in themselves and in the Lord was weakened by their divorce experience.

The length of time it takes for individuals to heal from such wounds depends largely on how soon and how completely they place their trust in the Savior and His promises. During the course of my conversations with these members, this led me to ask, "What is your understanding of the Atonement of Jesus Christ?" Their responses were usually *technically* accurate but did not evidence a personal *understanding* of the Savior's grace based on personal *experience* with it. It was apparent that most of these members did not yet trust that the power of Christ's Atonement could provide the strength and healing they so desperately needed.

In these situations, I would often express my hope that the loss of their *marriage* would not also lead to the loss of their *souls*, which happens to too many people that face serious adversity (see Matthew 16:26). At the moment of their greatest need, they turn away from instead of toward the *only* Source of stability and strength that can help them. Their pain creates a kind of perspective impairment that keeps them from seeing hope and joy as realistic possibilities for them anymore.

As I counseled with these members, I would explain that the plan of happiness had not changed just because their personal circumstances were now different. This life was still a testing period, and their journey would continue after death. Now, more than ever, they would need to draw strength and encouragement from the principles of forgiveness, repentance, humility, diligence, endurance, and charity. There would still be a final judgment and a celestial reward if they prepared themselves to receive it. The Lord's plan could yet lead to peace, rest, salvation, and eternal joy if they continued to pursue the course that leads to those blessings.

All of this was and is possible because there really was an Atonement.

Principles

Divorce is certainly not the only soul-stretching experience one can have in mortality. As we have already discussed, life is rife with a variety of tests and trials that can cause debilitating physical, emotional, or spiritual pain. The list of possibilities is endless.

Although the adverse circumstances we experience in this second estate are unique to each of us, what makes them the same is that they cause us to suffer. Let's face it, pain hurts and can weaken us regardless of its source. However, even though the degree of heartache or distress we feel during a trial may vary from one person to the next, the Source of our healing does not. The Source of healing varies neither by person nor the origin or depth of our travail.

Relief comes by trusting Jesus Christ, and that trust can be gained only by putting His promises to the test. The scriptures are replete with examples of the Savior inviting us to have confidence in His healing power and to learn why placing our trust in Him is desirable. Perhaps none is more encouraging than the invitation He extended to His disciples early on in His ministry:

> Come unto me, all ye that labour and are heavy laden, and
> I will give you rest.
>
> Take my yoke upon you, and learn of me; for I am meek and lowly in heart: and ye shall find rest unto your souls.
>
> For my yoke is easy, and my burden is light. (Matthew 11:28–30)

As indicated at the outset of this book, in our day, the Savior beckons us this way: "Learn of me, and listen to my words; walk in the meekness of my Spirit, and you shall have peace in me." (D&C 19:23)

Embedded in these and other entreaties Christ has offered are promised blessings to those who accept His invitation to come unto Him: "Ye shall find rest unto your souls" (Matthew 11:29) and "You shall have peace in me" (D&C 19:23). The scriptures likewise offer account after account of the Lord fulfilling the promises He has extended. Consider, for instance, this example as recounted by Elder Jeffrey R. Holland in a general conference address:

> On one occasion Jesus came upon a group arguing vehemently with His disciples. When the Savior inquired as to the cause of this contention, the father of an afflicted child stepped forward, saying he had approached Jesus's disciples for a blessing for his son, but they were not able to provide it. With the boy still gnashing his teeth, foaming from the mouth, and thrashing on the ground in front of them, the father appealed to Jesus with what must have been last-resort desperation in his voice:
>
> "If thou canst do any thing," he said, "have compassion on us, and help us.
>
> "Jesus said unto him, If thou canst believe, all things are possible to him that believeth.
>
> "And straightway the father of the child cried out, and said with tears, Lord, I believe; help thou mine unbelief."

This man's initial conviction, by his own admission, is limited. But he has an urgent, emphatic desire in behalf of his only child. We are told that is good enough for a beginning. "Even if ye can no more than *desire to believe*," Alma declares, "let this desire work in you, even until ye believe." With no other hope remaining, this father asserts what faith he has and pleads with the Savior of the world, "If *thou* canst do *any thing*, have compassion on *us*, and help *us*." I can hardly read those words without weeping. The plural pronoun *us* is obviously used intentionally. This man is saying, in effect, "Our whole family is pleading. Our struggle never ceases. We are exhausted. Our son falls into the water. He falls into the fire. He is continually in danger, and we are continually afraid. We don't know where else to turn. Can *you* help us? We will be grateful for *anything*—a partial blessing, a glimmer of hope, some small lifting of the burden carried by this boy's mother every day of her life."

"If *thou* canst do *any thing*," spoken by the father, comes back to him "If *thou* canst *believe*," spoken by the Master.

"Straightway," the scripture says—not slowly nor skeptically nor cynically but "straightway"—the father cries out in his unvarnished parental pain, "Lord, I believe; help thou mine unbelief." In response to new and still partial faith, Jesus heals the boy, almost literally raising him from the dead, as Mark describes the incident. (Jeffrey R. Holland, "Lord, I Believe," *Ensign*, May 2013.)

Any sincere seeker of the truth will find examples like this throughout the scriptures that testify of the help Christ promises and then delivers. We can readily find an abundance of evidence that He is true to His word—that He can be trusted. And those who engage in that kind of quest with pure intent quickly learn *through their own experience* what they can expect when they seek the Lord's guidance, comfort, and strength (see Moroni 10:3–5).

Given, then, what the Savior has made clear about His desire and ability to rescue us from our suffering, there is only one question remaining that we each must answer: "Do I trust Christ?"

Believing and trusting are not necessarily the same thing. I can believe my teenage son when he tells me things are going to be different now and he is not going to get any more tickets if I let him drive again. I can believe he has learned his lesson and is sincere about becoming a more careful driver. I can likewise believe *in* him—that he is capable of being a good driver and has all the talent and intelligence needed to become one. Having that belief, though, is not necessarily the same thing as *trusting* that he will be the good driver I *believe* he can be. However, that trust can be built over time as I grant him more opportunities to demonstrate his reliability and allow myself to accept that my belief in him is merited—because my *experience* with him is validating it.

Just to be clear, I am not suggesting that the burden is on the Savior to figure out how to earn our trust like a teenage son needs to earn the trust of his parents. Certainly, Christ's credibility is not on trial—ours is. The analogy merely serves to illustrate that there is a difference between trust and belief. Undoubtedly, if you ask a faithful Latter-day Saint if he or she believes in Christ, it is unlikely the response will be no. However, if that person has not had a *personal* experience with the healing power of the Savior's Atonement (or at least has been able to recognize a personal experience as such), then suggesting that they simply trust Christ is really not so . . . well, simple. In the teenage-driver analogy, if I have not yet had an experience that evidences my confidence in him is warranted, I may find it more difficult to trust him. Similarly, if members of the Church have not personally experienced or recognized atoning grace at work in their lives, they may find it difficult to truly put their trust in Christ. I think this is why there are so many members of the Church who believe *in* Christ—and even believe *Christ*—but still suffer unnecessarily.

To help us better understand how we can transform our belief into trust, let's look carefully at the words the Savior employs when He issues His invitation to lay claim on His promises of peace and rest. The terms He uses include *come, take, listen,* and *walk.* These words imply action. They are experience-centered words. The implication seems to be that as we move toward the Savior in accordance with His invitation and promises, He will *instill* greater trust within us. In other words, our *acts* of faith, however minor, make us eligible for the *gift* of faith. This is one of the lessons we learn from the interaction between the Savior and the distraught father who said, "Lord, I believe; help thou mine unbelief" (Mark 9:24). In our prayers, we might consider offering a similar plea when we, too, find ourselves stretched to the outer reaches of our belief.

We build our trust in the Savior by humbly following His teachings and keeping His commandments. Following a pattern of righteous living draws Christ's strength and healing endowment into our lives in the form of atoning grace (see Alma 38:9; D&C 19:23; Principle Five). And once grace is involved, we no longer need to rely on or operate under our own (limited) power. In another conference address, Elder Holland said it this way:

> He is saying to us, "Trust me, learn of me, do what I do. Then, when you walk where *I* am going," He says, "we can talk about where *you* are going, and the problems you face and the troubles you have. If you will follow me, I will lead you out of darkness," He promises. "I will give you answers to your prayers. I will give you rest to your souls." (Jeffrey R. Holland, "Broken Things to Mend," *Ensign*, May 2006.)

When faced with adversity, we need increased trust in the Savior. That increase will come as we apply the principles Elder Holland describes. It will also come as we focus on the truths we know and the past experiences we have had that evidence His love for us and how intimately He has been involved in our lives, as we discussed in chapter 2. Those truths and experiences remind us that there is reason to trust Christ. We can then build on that foundation as we attempt to navigate our present circumstance, just as I advised my grandsons to do if they ever again found themselves on an unfamiliar ski run during a raging storm.

Christ Completes Us

A critical point to make here is that Christ is not just a good and reliable source of comfort and relief when we are in pain. He is the *only* Source. Sometimes we act as though we wish there were an alternative route to peace and resolution that bypasses the Savior—perhaps one that does not demand too much of us. No such route exists (see Mosiah 3:17). More important, given what Christ has promised, why would we want or seek a different way? The Savior has the power to transform adversity into something that makes us spiritually complete and whole in an abiding manner and leads to sustained peace and rest (see 2 Nephi 2:1–2; D&C 121:7–8; D&C 122:7–9). Why would we choose a route that can at best only pacify us for the moment and more likely will make our situation worse?

Our cycles of despair will continue until we surrender to the truth that we cannot complete ourselves—spiritually, emotionally, or physically— any more than we can heal ourselves when we are sick or resurrect ourselves when we die. That is why a Savior is needed. And it is not a matter of Christ making up the difference between our efforts and what is actually needed to become spiritually whole. He paid the *full* price for our suffering so we do not have to. He made it possible for us to be complete, even perfect (see Moroni 10:32–33). But this can only happen by our demonstrating unmitigated trust in Him (see Jacob 4:8–11).

An Infinite but Personal Atonement

A key stumbling block that prevents many from fully trusting the Savior to provide needed relief and strength is the use of the term *infinite* in describing the scope of His Atonement. Because we cannot really comprehend what that word means or how it is measured, it is hard to accept that the Savior's Atonement has application or relevance to our daily lives. As a result, for many, it remains an abstract and somewhat discouraging concept rather than a comforting and empowering doctrine.

Overcoming this stumbling block requires a different perspective. We need to understand and accept that through the Atonement He performed, the Savior acquired two capacities: a divine empathy to be personally touched by every form of suffering we experience and the power to take *our* afflictions upon *Him* and replace them with strength, comfort, power, assurance, and peace. The word *infinite* is applied to Christ's propitiation because His Atonement granted Him a capacity without limits to its reach, either in the time period it covers or the issues it remedies. In that sense, *infinite* means Christ is able to *personalize* the succor He gives because His awareness of what we are experiencing is intimate, not general.

To make this principle a little clearer, let's equate this view of the infinite nature of Christ's Atonement with a real-life experience my spouse and I have had.

Both Mattie and I have lost our parents. Her father passed away first, in 1986, about three years after we were married. My father and mother passed away in 2000 within six months of each other. Fifteen years later, Mattie's mom passed away.

As each parent passed on, Mattie and I gained increased empathy for what the other was feeling. When my dad died, Mattie was able to intuit what that experience felt like for me, because she had been through it. Likewise, when her mom passed away, I had greater sensitivity to her feelings than I did when I learned of her father's death, because by then I had lost both of my parents.

The empathy my wife and I felt for each other in these circumstances was different from that experienced and expressed by friends and acquaintances who became aware of our losses. This is not because others were insincere in their sympathy. Rather, it is because Mattie and I knew each other more intimately than even our closest friends knew us. We each knew of each other's struggles, worries, joys, and ambitions and how the passing of a parent was affecting our partner in the context of our present experience. What we felt was a heightened and more personal kind of compassion than others could offer.

However, although Mattie and I shared an intimate empathy, we could not actually *feel* what the other was feeling—because we are separate and distinct beings. As a result, we could not perfectly respond to each other's needs, nor did we have the capacity to relieve or remove the grief our partner was experiencing. We could be sensitive, helpful, and attentive, but no mortal has the power to fill another person's emotional or spiritual void.

In contrast, through His vicarious Atonement, the Savior experienced the actual pain Mattie and I experienced when our parents passed away. He did not just know how we felt in some kind of generalized way, like the empathy my wife and I had for each other. He actually experienced our feelings in the full context of what was going on in our lives during those periods. He felt the weight of my grief being added to the career burdens I bore at that time and the worry I felt about whether I had done enough to help my parents in the months leading up to their passing. He felt Mattie's sorrow being heaped upon the pain and frustration she had experienced by not being able to spend more time with her mother before she died because we lived two states away. Beyond that, *Christ* assumed those burdens so they could be removed from *us*—so our suffering would not exceed its tutoring purpose and would have an end.

In performing His atoning act, Jesus also gained the power to replace whatever sorrow, worry, or anguish we experience with strength, courage, peace, comfort, and even joy. The same is true for every measure of temptation, sin, weakness, and difficulty—physical, spiritual, or emotional—any of us may encounter in our lives.

While the zenith of Christ's suffering occurred in the Garden of Gethsemane and on the cross, we must understand that His entire life was

LORD, HOW IS IT DONE? 39

a vicarious act *in our behalf.* When He said, "Take my yoke upon you . . . For my yoke is easy, and my burden is light" (Matthew 11:29–30), He was imploring us to believe that He has already assumed every burden we carry. He made it possible for the struggles we shoulder to be either lightened or removed *if* we will simply choose to replace our personal yoke with His—if we will trust Him.

I suppose this is why Paul taught that "we have not an high priest which cannot be touched with the feeling of our infirmities; but was in all points tempted like as we are, yet without sin" (Hebrews 4:15). After offering that reassurance, Paul issued this invitation: "Let us therefore come boldly unto the throne of grace, that we may obtain mercy, and find grace to help in time of need" (Hebrews 4:16).

I do not believe that by using the term *boldly* Paul intended to suggest we should approach the Lord *demandingly* when we seek His blessings. Rather, I think he was encouraging us to approach our Father with confidence that His Son understands with a comprehensive empathy every fear, worry, temptation, grief, sorrow, and affliction we experience and that He *has the ability to heal us* (see D&C 88:6; 122:8). Paul is saying that because of the unbounded and infinite nature of Christ's propitiation, when we approach the throne of grace, we will find relief.

Elder Holland provides an apt summary of these principles:

> It ought to be a matter of great doctrinal consolation to us that Jesus, in the course of the Atonement, experienced all of the heartache and sorrow, all of the disappointments and injustices that the entire family of man had experienced and would experience from Adam and Eve to the end of the world in order that we would not have to face them so severely or so deeply. However heavy our load might be, it would be a lot heavier if the Savior had not gone that way before us and carried that burden with us and for us. (Jeffrey R. Holland, "Lessons from Liberty Jail," *BYU Speeches*, September 2008.)

And so, as you attempt to confront the struggles before you, remember there is One who already bore those burdens for you; and He is worthy of your trust.

WHAT ENOS LEARNED

Behold, I went to hunt beasts in the forests; and the words which I had often heard
my father speak concerning eternal life, and the joy of the saints, sunk deep into my heart.
(Enos 1:3)

LIKE MANY MEMBERS OF THE Church today, Enos benefited from having a righteous heritage. His account implies he was raised in a strong family and was taught about the role Christ should play in his life (see Enos 1:1). It is hard to imagine it being otherwise, right? After all, Jacob was his father, Nephi was his uncle, and Lehi was his grandfather. With that pedigree, it is safe to assume he got a large dose of the truth and heard the doctrines of the gospel from an early age. In other words, it is unlikely Enos suffered a scarcity of spiritual training as he grew up.

And yet, despite that, he reached a point in this life when his soul hungered. In fact, the hunger was so severe that he "wrestled" in prayer before God all day and into the night in an effort to find relief (see Enos 1:4). Imagine what those hunger pains must have felt like (see James 1:3-7; Joseph Smith—History 1:10-20).

The day Enos spent in the forest came in the wake of some significant events in his life. He had been asked by his father to become the steward of the sacred record his family had been maintaining. Also around this time, his father passed away (see Jacob 7:27). Certainly, those kinds of sobering events would cause any of us to do some deep soul-searching. So were these the things that caused Enos's spiritual hunger? We simply don't know. More importantly, it really doesn't matter. What matters is that each of us can relate to what Enos was feeling. We all have moments of spiritual or emotional hunger. Life is difficult, and we often experience voids we are incapable of filling on our own. So it makes sense to learn from someone who has been there—someone who did not let that hollowness overcome him but instead took action to remedy it.

And what do we learn by observing Enos's response to his hunger? We learn how to satisfy it, not just in a temporary way but in a way that abides. We learn principles and doctrines that can help us *anytime* we hunger.

Although we don't know precisely what Enos was worried about or suffering from on his hunting excursion, we do know the things his father taught him had something to do with the hunger he was feeling. Apparently, he sensed there was a gap between the level of joy others experienced and his own. And, as evidenced by the steps he took in the wake of his pondering, he wanted to close that gap.

So where did he go for answers? Enos's own words tell us he went first to the truths he had been taught. "The words which I had often heard my father speak concerning eternal life, and the joy of the saints, sunk deep into my heart" (Enos 1:3). He allowed those truths to fuel his hope for something better ("the joy of the saints" [Enos 1:3]) and to guide the actions he took to relieve his struggles ("I kneeled down before my Maker" [Enos 1:4]). Because he ended up on his knees in his search for resolution, it is evident he had been taught about the purpose and efficacy of prayer (a subject addressed in more detail in chapter 11).

It is also evident that Enos's trust in the Lord had much to do with the result he received (see Enos 1:4–5). Much like the Prophet Joseph Smith, Enos seemed to know that his struggle could be resolved by talking to God about it (see Joseph Smith—History 1:11–15). But there was more to it than that. It is apparent Enos knew God was the *only* one who could resolve his dilemma. Why else would he endure in prayer for so long? It seems he knew that whatever he was wrestling with was not going to be resolved through any other means. Perhaps he had tried and exhausted all other avenues prior to that day in the woods. It is also apparent that in the process of seeking help from above, he knew he could not simply make a perfunctory request of God. Nor should he instruct God about when his

answer should come or what it should be (see Jacob 4:8–
10). He seemed to have learned that the Lord expected
him to engage in some serious introspection, even to
the point of wrestling (see James 1:3–10). This was the
same lesson Joseph Smith learned, and coincidentally, his
experience, like Enos's, also occurred in a grove of trees.

In the end, Enos was rewarded for envisioning the possibilities. He did not surrender to his feelings or abandon
his hope when things got difficult. He allowed truth and
perspective to guide him. As a result, what he hoped for
and envisioned came true.

Assessment

To help you determine the extent to which you are able to Envision the
Possibilities (see Principle One), consider completing this brief assessment.
Give each statement a score between 1 and 10 (10 suggesting the statement
describes you completely) based on your current state of mind and circumstances. Your scores will help you identify strengths you can build upon and
barriers you need to address as you seek to overcome challenges and make
spiritual progress.

1. I feel in control of my future and know what steps I need to take to
   overcome my present condition.
2. I know where and how to find truth.
3. I believe I am a person of divine heritage, worth, and potential.
4. I associate regularly with others who know the truth of who they
   really are.
5. I resist the temptation to be discouraged, depressed, or pessimistic
   about my future.
6. I desire to be happy.
7. I trust Jesus Christ and live my life in accordance with the faith I
   have in Him.

8. I accept that I cannot overcome the challenges of mortality without the Atonement of Jesus Christ.
9. I currently feel love and reassurance from Heavenly Father and the Savior.
10. I have experienced the Atonement of Jesus Christ in my life.

As you review your scores, which areas represent strengths you can build upon? Which are areas that could become potential barriers to your peace if not addressed?

Strengths to Build Upon:
  1.
  2.
  3.

Potential Barriers to Peace:
  1.
  2.
  3.

Consider making notes about the steps you plan to take to improve your application of this principle.

Actions:
  1.
  2.
  3.

PRINCIPLE TWO

BUILD A STRONG FOUNDATION

And now, my sons, remember, remember that it is upon the rock of our Redeemer, who is Christ, the Son of God, that ye must build your foundation; that when the devil shall send forth his mighty winds, yea, his shafts in the whirlwind, yea, when all his hail and his mighty storm shall beat upon you, it shall have no power over you to drag you down to the gulf of misery and endless wo, because of the rock upon which ye are built, which is a sure foundation, a foundation whereon if men build they cannot fall.
(Helaman 5:12; emphasis added)

This verse from Helaman is one of many that could be shared about the importance of constructing the right foundation as we pursue spiritual victory in mortality. Certainly, as Helaman states, Christ is the foundation upon which we must build. Learning how to increase our trust in Him is essential to having an experience with His Atonement. Yet, the title question of this book remains: "Lord, how is it done? How do I form and preserve the 'sure foundation' to which Helaman refers?"

The foundation is that part of a building upon which the structure depends for stability. The word *foundation* is also used to describe the spiritual underpinnings we must develop if our spiritual structure is going to be stable. Unfortunately, too often our lives are built on a shifting foundation. We are governed by our emotions, what others think of us, what is trending and popular, or other things "which man's wisdom teacheth" (1 Corinthians 2:13). For some, there is no foundation at all. As a result, when mortality serves up its relentless series of challenges and tests, they become vulnerable because there is nothing in place to hold up their spiritual structure. This is why some feel like their life is crumbling beneath them, because in a very real sense, it is.

This section addresses this issue by discussing how we can build and sustain a strong spiritual foundation in our lives. It is essentially a how-to guide for all who want secure footing as they pursue an abiding experience with the Savior's Atonement. We cannot bypass or ignore the principles taught in this section and expect to experience the fruit of atoning grace and the peace it promises.

CHAPTER 4
Follow Righteous Patterns

In a revelation given through the Prophet Joseph Smith in June of 1831, the Lord declared, 'I will give unto you a pattern in all things, that ye may not be deceived; for Satan is abroad in the land, and he goeth forth deceiving the nations' (D&C 52:14). I invite you to consider a specific phrase in this verse—'a pattern in all things' . . . Patterns help to avoid waste and unwanted deviations and facilitate uniformity that is appropriate and beneficial . . .Vital spiritual patterns are evident in the life of the Savior, in the scriptures, and in the teachings of living prophets and apostles. These spiritual patterns are now and always have been important aids to discernment and sources of direction and protection for faithful Latter-day Saints. (David A. Bednar, "By Small and Simple Things are Great Things Brought to Pass," BYU Women's Conference, April 2011.)

KEY UNDERSTANDING 4
Spiritual healing, strength, capacity, progress, and confidence are byproducts of righteous patterns.

Daily Life

When Matt, a shy young man about to turn sixteen years old, came to visit with me, he was about to take a major step in his life. On the following Saturday, he would be baptized, along with his mother and sister. Matt had been somewhat adrift up to this point in his life. As his mother would later tell me, she and his father used to worry about Matt because of his lack of ambition and general resistance to responsibility.

Because I was about to become Matt's bishop, he and I were meeting to talk about the step he was taking and what it meant. After discussing his impending baptism, we shifted our attention to the priesthood. I spoke with him about Heavenly Father's plan for sharing His authority and how all worthy males over the age of twelve were eligible to receive it. We talked about Matt's opportunity to receive the Aaronic Priesthood, and I taught him about the responsibilities he would assume as a priest, as well as the blessings that would come through his service.

As this part of our discussion progressed, it became apparent Matt was uneasy. Ultimately, he told me he did not feel ready to take such a step. His concern was rooted in a natural reluctance toward responsibility combined with his newfound understanding of the significance of the ordination. He was taking it seriously and did not want to commit to a role he was not sure he could properly fulfill. As a result, Matt asked if he could think about it for a while and maybe revisit the subject again sometime after his baptism. By "sometime," it was clear to me he hoped the issue would just kind of fade away so he would not have to deal with it.

I hasten to point out that Matt's reluctance had nothing to do with his testimony or worthiness. During our interview, it was apparent Matt had felt something significant while taking the missionary lessons and was compelled by the truths he was being taught. He had received a spiritual witness. We likewise talked about what it meant to be worthy to hold the priesthood— and he was meeting that standard. But baptism was already a big step; it was going to require a large dose of courage for Matt to walk into the font on Saturday afternoon. And receive the priesthood too? Well, that was too much too soon.

So we agreed to revisit the subject later but proceed with his baptism that weekend.

Following his baptism, Matt entered the stream of activity that Church membership encourages: Sunday meetings, priesthood quorum involvement, youth activities, seminary, family home evening, and so on. In addition, prayer and scripture study became part of his daily routine. He fully surrendered to all the behavioral patterns his new faith encouraged.

Matt had the good fortune of participating in a large priests quorum and youth program with outstanding young men and women who embraced and included him. Most of his quorum members wore a suit, white shirt, and tie on Sundays. Fewer than three years later, fifteen of those young men were in the mission field at the same time. You get the picture—it was a magical environment for a young new convert. However, none of that magic would have rubbed off on Matt had he not developed the spiritual habits that consistently kept him exposed to those positive influences.

About a month after his baptism, Matt found himself back in the bishop's office revisiting the subject of the Aaronic Priesthood. His reluctance had not completely vanished, but he was more trusting now. He was willing to take a leap of faith and be ordained, hoping God would make him equal to the task. And God did.

In the weeks and months that followed, a miraculous transformation occurred in Matt. He began attending church dressed like his fellow priests quorum members. (His mother caught him in front of a bedroom mirror one day admiring himself in his new suit, white shirt, and tie. "I'm just seeing what I'll look like as a missionary," he said.) He blessed the sacrament. His countenance changed, and he carried a perpetual smile on his face. He served as secretary in the priests quorum presidency. On multiple fast Sundays and in youth conferences, he stood to bear his testimony. There was an obvious spiritual maturing taking place in Matt, and we all could see it.

Other parts of Matt's life got better as well. His grades improved in school. He ran track and cross-country. He spent time with his family and set an example for his younger sister. He was likewise an influence for good on his fellow quorum members.

Following high school, Matt was admitted to BYU–Idaho. There, among other curricula, he attended mission preparation classes. Letters and calls home revealed a very different young man than the once ambivalent teenager whose parents had worried about his future.

Soon, a mission call arrived. Matt was called to serve in the Mexico Puebla Mission. After a conversation with her son on his second Mother's Day in the field, his mom's Facebook post told the whole story:

> Best hour ever!!!! Spoke with my 20-year-old son in Mexico for an hour. His Spanish is great as far as I can tell. He occasionally exchanged a Spanish word for an English word while talking to us today. Sometimes he would catch himself; other times, until I started laughing, he didn't know. Eight more months till he comes home, and he says he wants to stay an additional year. Lucky for me, they don't let him extend that long! (Colleen Stuver Christensen, Facebook post, date unknown)

Matt finished his mission honorably, returned to BYU–Idaho, met his future bride, and got married in the temple.

Principles

As you read Matt's story, what do you conclude? What accounts for his transformation? How did a shy, reluctant teenager mature so quickly into a self-assured young man filled with confidence, vision, commitment, testimony, influence, and the Spirit?

The answer is found in the spiritual patterns he made part of his life. His transformation began when he engaged in the first principles and ordinances of the gospel and then accelerated as he embraced all of the practices and routines associated with gospel living (see 2 Nephi 31:20–21). He first observed those patterns at work in others' lives and then adopted them in his own life.

In the quote that begins this chapter, Elder Bednar suggests the word *pattern* refers to activities that are repeated and renewed with regularity. In a gospel context, the term connotes steadfastness in righteous behavior (see 2 Nephi 31:20). By deliberately pursuing spiritual habits, over time we bear the fruits of increased hope, broadened and more inspired perspective, and deepened faith. Our engagement in spiritual patterns invites the Lord to educate our desires and nourish our spirits. Once we secure the partnership of the Savior through our diligence, grace is activated in our lives. In time, grace's power becomes an abiding force of such magnitude that righteous behavior is almost inevitable. This is what happened for Matt.

Spiritual patterns also keep us from being deceived by the adversary (see D&C 10:5–7, 20, 22–27). They ensure that we are able to see the path of truth more clearly and discern Satan's counterfeit claims. In the scripture quoted by Elder Bednar, the Lord tells us: "I will give unto you a pattern in all things, *that ye may not be deceived*" (D&C 52:14, emphasis added). By following the behaviors the Lord modeled and advocated, we create a secure foundation upon which a life of righteousness can be built and can mature—one that will hold us up when life's storms beat upon us.

When we feel spiritually and emotionally unsettled or drained, it is usually because we have departed from one or more patterns of righteousness. Because that is true, we should consider the spiritual habits and practices upon which an experience with Christ's Atonement is facilitated. Although a multitude of righteous patterns could be discussed, here we will focus on the four I believe are the root of all others.

DAILY SCRIPTURE STUDY AND PRAYER

A wise former bishop of mine used to pose a simple question to those who came to him about serious problems or sinful practices they were engaged in. He would ask, "How many times in the last seven days have you studied the scriptures and had personal prayer?" It will not surprise you that the responses were almost always, "Zero." Some were confused and others even offended by the question, wondering how it was relevant to the issue they had come to discuss. Here are three scriptural references (among many that could be mentioned) that evidence the relevance of this bishop's question:

"Feast upon the words of Christ; for behold, the words of Christ *will tell you all things what ye should do.*" (2 Nephi 32:3, emphasis added)

"If any of you lack wisdom, *let him ask of God,* that giveth to all men liberally, and upbraideth not; and it shall be given him." (James 1:5, emphasis added)

"Draw near unto me and I will draw near unto you; *seek* me diligently and ye shall find me; *ask,* and ye shall receive; *knock,* and it shall be opened unto you." (D&C 88:63, emphases added)

I suspect the application of those three scriptural directives alone would solve most of the problems we encounter in life and pull us out of the spiritual mire in which we often find ourselves. That was the bishop's point in asking the question. But, please note, these verses do not suggest that a casual approach to scripture study and prayer will suffice. Instead, the Lord emphasizes that diligence and commitment will be necessary. That is why the practices of scripture study and prayer need to become patterns in our lives, not just occasional activities.

"Feasting" implies a serious investment in learning the word, not just sampling spiritual hors d'oeuvres periodically without ever really partaking of the main course. And the verse in James does not say, "If any of you lack *information,* let him ask of God." It says, "If any of you lack *wisdom,* let him ask of God." Our feasting for *information* enables the Lord to fill us with His *wisdom* when we plead for direction, comfort, or healing because we have prepared our minds and hearts for the counsel He wants to give. Similarly, the terms "seek," "ask," and "knock" are not passive in nature. They suggest the Lord expects us to make a sustained and sincere effort to learn His will and then follow the direction He gives us (see D&C 84:44–46). I suspect Enos would endorse such an approach. His diligent application of this pattern resulted in an experience with the Savior's Atonement that completely resolved his spiritual hunger. The same can be true for you and me if we will make prayer and scripture study a daily practice.

Listening and Hearkening to the *Right* Voices

Every day, each of us is exposed to a variety of voices that compete for our attention. As we go about our routines, we *hear* many things without any election on our part. However, what we *listen* to is different. Listening is a deliberate choice we make. For example:

- We *choose* those with whom we will engage in conversation.
- We *choose* what kind of music we will listen to.
- We *choose* to either pay attention to the messages delivered by the speakers and teachers on Sundays or spend that time scrolling through our cell phones.
- When general conference is held, we *choose* to either tune in and listen or to devote our time and attention elsewhere.

The reason our listening choices are so important is because divine communication is modestly presented. It is not flamboyant or brazen. We have to seek it out.

Unfortunately, many of us have not formed a pattern of nurturing the channels through which spiritual messages come. We are too preoccupied with the mists of darkness represented by the voices of the world to engage in activities that will lead us to the tree of life (see 1 Nephi 8:10–11; 23). Those who render themselves spiritually deaf in this manner fail to recognize that there are messages and messengers available to help them in their times of struggle, but those messages and messengers must be invited in. They will not impose themselves on us.

This principle was at work during the experience the Nephites had when the Father introduced Christ to them just prior to the Savior's descent into their midst. The record explains,

> They heard a voice as if it came out of heaven; and they
> cast their eyes round about, *for they understood not the voice*
> *which they heard*; and it was not a harsh voice, neither was
> it a loud voice; nevertheless, and notwithstanding it being
> a small voice it did pierce them that did hear to the center.
> (3 Nephi 11:3, emphasis added)

They heard the voice a second time but "understood it not" (3 Nephi 11:4). And then we read how the Nephites were finally able to understand the voice they had been hearing:

> And again the third time they did *hear* the voice, and *did*
> *open their ears to hear it; and their eyes were towards the*
> *sound thereof;* and *they did look steadfastly towards heaven,*
> from whence the sound came.
> And behold, *the third time they did understand the voice*
> *which they heard*; and it said unto them:
> Behold my Beloved Son, in whom I am well pleased,
> in whom I have glorified my name—hear ye him. (3 Nephi
> 11:5–7, emphases added)

Note the effort the Nephites had to make before they *understood* the voice they had been *hearing*. Once they proactively engaged in *listening*, understanding came, and they were ready to greet the Savior.

During His earthly ministry, Christ similarly exhorted His followers to be more deliberate in their listening. After teaching the parable of the sower He admonished, "Who hath ears to hear, *let him hear*" (Matthew 13:9; emphasis added). These examples and others from the scriptures suggest that finding and listening to the *right* voices cannot be a passive effort if we want this pattern to yield fruit.

DEVELOPING AN OBEDIENCE REFLEX

The natural extension of learning truth, through the patterns just described, is acting on the knowledge we gain. And to receive a full measure of the Savior's grace, we must make hearkening to the truth a reflex. In other words, if we want to gain enduring access to the empowerment Christ is willing to provide, especially during challenging times, we must learn to nurture our spiritual sensitivities to the point that obedience becomes as automatic to us as breathing.

Our challenge with this pattern is that, unlike the built-in reflexes our body has, *spiritual* reflexes have to be deliberately cultivated. Among other things, this implies we must learn to routinely subordinate our emotions and impulses to a more elevated response that leads us to obey *first*, rather than to challenge or rebel. This kind of reflex is developed by consistently following revealed patterns of conduct and thought that align our way of thinking and acting with the Lord's way and order (see 1 Corinthians 2:16). Persistent engagement in the practices of scripture study, prayer, and hearkening to the right voices is essential.

So how do we know if our obedience reflex is fully developed?

Our propensity to obey is revealed in the way we respond to inspired instruction from the Lord. For example, some, when hearing counsel from Church leaders, receive that direction with a spirit of casualness and sometimes even rebellion. They demonstrate little urgency to make changes in their lives or to surrender their will to the guidance given. Consequently, they restrict the Lord's ability to bestow certain blessings because they do not receive the counsel He is offering (see Jacob 4:8–10; D&C 84:36–37). Of such the Lord has said,

> They were slow to hearken unto the voice of the Lord their God; therefore, the Lord their God is slow to hearken unto their prayers, to answer them in the day of their trouble.
>
> In the day of their peace they esteemed lightly my counsel; but, in the day of their trouble, of necessity they feel after me. (D&C 101:7–8)

Developing a pattern of listening to and obeying those who have priesthood keys brings about a meekness and submissiveness that alters our spiritual perspective (see David A. Bednar, "Meek and Lowly in Heart," *Ensign*, April 2018). This strengthens our capacity to receive more counsel as it comes—because obedience magnifies our hearkening reflexes (see D&C 84:45–47). By following this pattern, a spiritual virtuous cycle is formed that perpetuates and sustains our ability to be strengthened and empowered *regularly* by the Savior and to recognize the tender mercies He consistently offers. Virtuous cycles are behaviors or systems that perpetuate good outcomes and accelerate growth. Hence, the more we obey, the stronger our spiritual virtuous cycle becomes.

Spending our Time and Means on That Which is Good

How we use our time and means either protects us spiritually or makes us vulnerable. It is clear that Satan and his allies want to persuade us to make choices that ultimately limit our freedom and enslave us to our passions, appetites, and selfish tendencies (see Mosiah 3:19). As a result, it is critical that we develop activity habits that provide a spiritual shield. This means we must deliberately seek out and nurture opportunities that invite more light into our lives while consciously rejecting pursuits and pastimes that can ensnare us in destructive patterns (see Principle Four).

Our mortal experience is essentially an extended battle between light and darkness (see 2 Nephi 2:11). However, darkness can wield power over us only if we invite it into our lives. We either invite or reject its influence by how we spend our time. And the more we engage in activities that impair our spiritual senses, the harder it becomes to recognize the difference between light and darkness, good and evil, or whether something is right or wrong.

With these opposing forces in mind, Mormon offered clear direction about how to determine which activities will draw light into our lives:

> But behold, that which is of God inviteth and enticeth to do good continually; wherefore, every thing which inviteth and enticeth to do good, and to love God, and to serve him, is inspired of God. . . .
>
> For every thing which inviteth . . . to persuade to believe in Christ, is sent forth by the power and gift of Christ; wherefore ye may know with a perfect knowledge it is of God. . . .
>
> Wherefore, I beseech of you, brethren, that ye should search diligently in the light of Christ that ye may know good from evil; and if ye will lay hold upon every good thing, and condemn it not, ye certainly will be a child of Christ. (Moroni 7:13, 16, 19)

Note some of the criteria Mormon mentions as approved activities for developing the correct patterns in the use of our time. They are those things that invite (encourage) us "to do good" and to "believe in Christ." That is pretty straightforward counsel.

The Lord has further clarified what is good and will persuade us "to believe in Christ" as follows:

> We believe in being honest, true, chaste, benevolent, virtu-
> ous, and in doing good to all men . . . If there is anything
> virtuous, lovely, or of good report or praiseworthy, *we seek*
> *after these things.* (Articles of Faith 1:13, emphasis added)

Mormon's inspired instruction, coupled with Joseph Smith's declaration in the thirteenth article of faith, offer uncomplicated guidance to anyone hoping to receive a greater endowment of atoning grace in times of difficulty. We simply need to compare our current use of time with those criteria and see what gaps or conflicts exist. In particular, note the closing phrase in the thirteenth article of faith: "we seek after these things." That statement implies we should *actively* pursue good and edifying activities. We cannot simply wait for "these things" to come to us, because we are constantly bombarded by the devices the devil uses to distract and confuse. We must deliberately choose good activities over other, less-elevating ones.

Here are just a few examples of the kinds of choices we might make if we are proactively trying to pursue that which is "virtuous, lovely, or of good report or praiseworthy":

- Increased temple attendance over increased recreational activity
- Deepened Sabbath day observance over catching up on work projects
- Increased reading time (especially scripture reading) over increased TV time
- Devotion to service (including in our callings) instead of to additional personal indulgences
- Complete honesty in our payment of tithes and generosity in our fast offerings instead of increased consumption of the newest and most popular thing, whatever it might be
- Increased time interacting with family members and decreased time on social media
- Participation in missionary service instead of getting through school earlier or indulging in the free time retirement offers

Certainly, more choices could be added to this list. Through humble self-examination, other opportunities to improve the use of our time and means will manifest themselves in a personalized way. And this is certainly something we can consult with the Lord about in prayer. He will guide and direct us to know where we need to improve (see Matthew 19:20–21).

It has been my experience that as we engage in the four patterns just described, we will find ourselves naturally drawn to related spiritual habits. Daily scripture reading and prayer also lead us to engage in a meaningful fast—and not just on the first Sunday of the month but whenever we are faced with issues requiring greater light and heavenly direction or comfort. Proactively seeking out the right voices leads us to be where those voices can be heard (e.g., our Sunday church meetings, stake conference, general conference, *Come, Follow Me* study with our families, and edifying conversations in our homes). Reflexive obedience makes us more sensitive to spiritual promptings that come from the Holy Ghost, directing us how to act in *all* that we do (see 2 Nephi 32:2–3). And the consecration of our time and means makes priorities clearer and turns our hearts and minds to the things that matter most in our lives—our relationship with our Heavenly Father and our relationship with each other. All of these patterns lead us to "walk in the light, as he is in the light" and "have fellowship with" the Savior so "the blood of Jesus Christ [can cleanse] us from all sin" (1 John 1:7).

CHAPTER 5

Proceed with Faith

When faith is properly understood and used, it has dramatically far-reaching effects. Such faith can transform an individual's life from maudlin, common everyday activities to a symphony of joy and happiness. The exercise of faith is vital to Father in Heaven's plan of happiness. But true faith, faith unto salvation, is centered on the Lord Jesus Christ, faith in His doctrines and teachings, faith in the prophetic guidance of the Lord's anointed, faith in the capacity to discover hidden characteristics and traits that can transform life. Truly, faith in the Savior is a principle of action and power.
(*Richard G. Scott, "The Transforming Power of Faith and Character,"* Ensign, *November 2010.*)

KEY UNDERSTANDING 5
Faith is a principle of action that enlivens our hope and grants us access to atoning grace. That grace endows us with the power to conquer adversity and temptation and remain steadfast in righteousness. Our righteousness is subsequently rewarded with an additional outpouring of the gift of faith (see 2 Nephi 31:20).

Daily Life

As Didi, a sixteen-year-old young woman in our ward, made her way to the front of the room, there was a palpable reverence among those attending the youth testimony meeting that was underway. All eyes were fixed on this blonde, curly haired girl who stood to speak. Everyone was aware that Didi had undergone a life-altering event that week, so they were especially focused on what she had to say.

Given the circumstances, it took an extra measure of courage for Didi just to be there, no less stand before her peers on that occasion. Quite frankly, I had not expected to see her family at church that Sunday. Didi's mom had lost her battle with cancer just a few days prior. There had been long, painful weeks leading up to her passing, and the grief had been unbearable for Didi, her siblings, and her father. No one would have faulted them for sitting it out and staying home. That Sunday's special testimony meeting for the young men and young women culminated the just-concluded Newport Beach California Temple open house, youth celebration, and dedication. Those events had been richly edifying. As a result, the youth were filled to their spiritual brims when it came time to share their testimonies about their experiences.

Didi had participated in all the temple events, despite many demands and concerns at home as her mother entered her final days. To attend the temple dedicatory session on the previous Sunday, Didi and her family had left their mom in the care of a hospice worker—hoping and trusting she would still be alive when they returned home. At the session they attended, six seats became available in one of the sealing rooms. Didi, her three sisters, her father, and her brother-in law were invited to sit there. The significance of that opportunity under those circumstances was lost on no one.

It seemed nothing short of a miracle that the Newport Beach California Temple events paralleled the difficult but sacred season occurring in Didi's family's life. The mirrored timing of those events made the veil very thin. In particular, Didi's participation in the youth celebration gave her a unique perspective about her family's circumstances, something that would become apparent as she shared her testimony.

I made some notes during the meeting as Didi and others spoke. Although I do not consider what follows to be a verbatim account of what she said, I believe it captures the essence of Didi's remarks that day during her testimony. Here, in part, are her comments as recorded in the notes I made:

> When we were practicing for the temple celebration, it was hard for me to visualize what we were creating. During rehearsals, I couldn't see what it looked like from up above, where the audience would be sitting. Sometimes it was frustrating because of that. I had to trust that those who were directing us knew how it would turn out.

I now have to likewise trust that my Heavenly Father can see things from where He sits that I can't see. I know He will make something beautiful out of this situation, just as He did with the youth performance. I know He has given me this trial because I can handle it and need to learn from it.

I am so grateful for the temple. When we went there for the dedication, we sat in the sealing room. I know there were angels there.

Didi then bore testimony of the Savior and His Atonement and expressed gratitude for the gospel and the Church. She expressed love for her family, friends, and leaders. She also paid tribute to her mother.

It was a singular moment and one of the clearest perspectives on faith I had ever heard. I suspect others who listened to Didi that day felt the same way.

Principles

Often, our faith is weaker than it should be in light of the many evidences the Lord has given for why we can trust Him. This reality usually manifests itself when a major trial or temptation comes. In other words, we *think* we have faith until our faith is tested. I believe this happens primarily because we don't fully understand the principle.

What we can learn from Didi's example is that our understanding of faith comes through experiment and experience, just as our understanding of the Savior's Atonement comes through experiment and experience. We cannot comprehend faith fully through study alone, because faith is a spiritual gift that is *bestowed* on those willing to test the Lord's promises. By *test* I mean we commit to obeying God's laws *before* we have received the blessings we are seeking, and we continue in obedience even when the hoped-for outcome is not immediately granted. In short, obedience is an *act* of faith that is rewarded with the Lord's *gift* of faith.

As discussed in the previous chapter, faith-fueled obedience sets a spiritual virtuous cycle in motion. As we increase our obedience, our faith in Christ also increases (because we are granted the *gift* of faith). The fruit of our effort is knowledge, the attainment of which Alma said tastes "delicious" (see Alma 32:28). Because that experience is so joyful, we become naturally inclined toward more obedience, which in turn perpetuates and increases the sweet assurances (additional light and knowledge) our Savior grants to reward our faith. This is how faith initiated by *experiment* can grow into knowledge that is obtained by *experience*.

Given faith's role in our gaining access to atoning grace, it is critical that we learn how to obtain and sustain this gift. Perhaps this learning is best initiated by first assessing the current state or condition of our faith. Once we are clear-eyed in our self-assessment, we can take the necessary steps to *increase* our faith.

Taking Our Faith Temperature

So how do we perform this kind of assessment? How might we measure the level of our faith?

Typically, the depth of our faith is revealed in the patterns of thought and behavior we engage in routinely. Too often, our attitude and the self-talk we allow in response to our life circumstances erode rather than promote faith. When we permit a negative or pessimistic thought process to become entrenched in our minds, our spiritual growth is stifled, and we are prevented from experiencing a greater measure of the Savior's grace and seeing the tender mercies He regularly extends (see 1 Nephi 1:20).

To make this clearer, let's look at two contrasting lists of thoughts and behaviors we might adopt in our lives. On the left side of the chart below are attributes and tendencies that weaken our faith. On the right side are those that strengthen it. Perhaps this list can be used to help us determine the state of our faith at present. Ask yourself which terms best describe your self-talk and the outlook you have right now.

WEAKENING FAITH	STRENGTHENING FAITH
Murmuring or complaining	Being cheerful and uplifting
Pessimism	Optimism
Being dismissive	Being open
Stubbornness	Submissiveness
Pride	Humility
Being judgmental	Praising others

WEAKENING FAITH	STRENGTHENING FAITH
Ignoring or dismissing priesthood direction	Seeking priesthood counsel
Disobedience	Steadfastness
Anger	Forgiveness
Acting entitled	Showing gratitude
Self-pity	Unselfishness
Finding joy in others' misfortune	Expressing compassion
Envy	Acceptance
Victimhood	Taking Responsibility
Impatience	Endurance
Wishful thinking	Being proactive
Withdrawal	Engagement
Despair	Hope
Iniquity	Repentance

If the terms that resonate with you most right now are on the Weakening Faith side of the chart, well . . . you are probably pretty normal. Unfortunately, normal is not helpful if you need faith that is strong enough to meet and overcome the challenges before you. So what should you do?

For each of us, the first step is to look at this exercise as a wake-up call. By honestly assessing our current condition, we can catch ourselves before we descend into deeper cycles of despair and hopelessness that erode our faith. Based on the insight this review gives us, we can start forming better faith *habits* by incorporating the kinds of responses and self-talk listed on the Strengthening Faith side of the chart. Then we can begin more fully immersing ourselves in the *process* of faith, learning and applying the revealed steps that will transition us from a state of weakening *belief* to one of hope-filled *action* that draws the powers of heaven into our lives.

The Process of Faith

A process is typically thought of as a series of defined steps or actions that help us produce or sustain a result we want to achieve or perpetuate. Processes provide structure, direction, and efficiency. They allow us to envision *how* we can actually attain the thing we are pursuing, whatever it might be. We embrace good processes because they enable us to translate mere ideas into actionable steps that produce tangible outcomes. Good processes eliminate guesswork and offer a clear path for us to follow.

Perhaps it is for this reason that, in the restored gospel, God has revealed a multitude of processes designed to enable our spiritual progress and success. Preparing for and receiving ordinances is a process. Making and keeping covenants is a process. Repentance is a process. Sabbath day adherence and temple worship are processes. And faith is a process.

By following divinely prescribed methods, we can enlist the Savior as our partner in pursuing an inspired solution to our struggles. This allows the source of our strength to become Jesus Christ Himself. That strength is manifest in the endowment of grace He extends to those who place their trust in Him. And because revealed processes lay out a clear path we can follow, they imbue us with confidence that we will achieve the result we are seeking. They show us each step we need to take toward the proverbial light at the end of the tunnel.

In life, many of us fail to make the progress we seek because we do not fully understand how the process of faith works or the steps it includes. As a result, when difficulties come, we are unsure of the next action we should initiate to make progress. This uncertainty can paralyze us spiritually. It is what causes many to fall into cycles of despair.

Faith requires us to act *before* we know or experience what a future outcome might be. We act on our hope that the Savior's promises will be fulfilled in our behalf if we follow true principles and revealed patterns. As such, it is critical that we gain a clear understanding of what the *process* of faith entails (see Alma 32:21; Ether 12:6). Then, whenever we are faced with a challenge or decision that requires us to act without knowing what lies ahead, we can identify where we are in the faith process and what we need to do next.

Eight-Step Faith Process

By using the term *process* to describe how faith is obtained or increased, I do not mean to suggest that a principle this profound can be mastered by simply following a list of to-dos. As already stated, faith is a gift that is bestowed upon those who persevere in righteousness. However, the scriptures on the subject do imply that the first principle of the gospel has an evolutionary nature to it and that there are things we can and must do to give that evolution momentum and unlock its stabilizing power (see Alma 32:26–43). Here, I have organized that progression into eight steps or phases that I am calling the faith process. Each step builds and relies on the one before it. By looking at the development of faith this way, we can more easily pinpoint where we are now and what we need to do next to strengthen our faith.

Step One: Hear and Receive the Word of Truth

So then faith cometh by hearing, and hearing by the word of God.
(Romans 10:17)

The starting point in developing faith is hearing truth (see D&C 93:24; D&C 84:45). Therefore, if we want our faith to grow, we must make sure we are frequently putting ourselves in a position to hear the word of God. This means we will need to become more selective about the voices we let influence us, decreasing exposure to those that weaken our faith and increasing exposure to those that can strengthen it. If our faith is in a vulnerable state, or early on in its evolution, we need the nourishment only consistent immersion in truth can provide (see 1 Nephi 17:3; Moroni 6:4).

But merely hearing the word is not enough. We must also proactively listen and wholeheartedly receive the word. Nephi taught, "When a man speaketh by the power of the Holy Ghost the power of the Holy Ghost carrieth it *unto* the hearts of the children of men" (2 Nephi 33:1, emphasis added). In other words, the Holy Ghost will deliver truth to us, but He will not force us to accept or apply it. The truth He delivers is of no real value if we do not allow it to affect us. Whether or not we have "received" the word is evidenced by the actions we take after hearing it (see D&C 84:46).

When we allow ourselves to more consistently hear—that is, listen and hearken to—the word of the Lord, and open our hearts to receive it, we are initiating the evolution of our faith.

Step Two: Desire to Believe

And it came to pass after I, Nephi, having heard all the words of my father, concerning the things which he saw in a vision, and also the things which he spake by the power of the Holy Ghost . . . I, Nephi, was desirous also that I might see, and hear, and know of these things.
(1 Nephi 10:17; emphases added; see also Step One in the process of faith)

When we allow the Spirit to penetrate our hearts with truth, something happens to our desires. This is because truth makes us see things differently and instills hope (see Alma 31:5; Ether 12:4). As indicated in the verse just referenced, such was Nephi's experience after he heard his father describe his vision of the tree of life. This kind of deep spiritual yearning helps us to begin envisioning something better, richer, fuller, clearer, happier, or perhaps just more stable than what we are currently experiencing (see Hebrews 11:1; Enos 1:3–4). Such inspired expectancy—which is really just hope in embryo—is what truth produces in an open heart (see John 16:13; D&C 6:15).

As we allow the truth to penetrate our hearts in even a small measure, the Light of Christ responds by igniting something within our spirits. That light is a compelling force. It is so compelling that exposure to it usually results in a feeling of spiritual unrest until we respond to what the light is encouraging us to do (see D&C 84:45–46). That experience creates a kind of tug-of-war between hope and despair and gives birth to an increased desire for more light and truth. It is that simple desire that allows our faith to take root and leads us to experiment on the word.

Step Three: Experiment on the Word

But behold, if ye will awake and arouse your faculties, even to an experiment upon my words, and exercise a particle of faith, *yea, even if ye can no more than* desire to believe, *let this desire work in you, even until ye believe in a manner that ye can give place for a portion of my words.*
(Alma 32:27; emphases added)

In science, experimentation is the means by which a hypothesis is tested. By performing the experiment, scientists determine if their belief is viable—if it can be validated. In spiritual matters, the Savior has taught that the same principle applies: "If any man will do his will, he shall know of the doctrine, whether it be of God, or whether I speak of myself" (see John 7:17). If that is true, how do we properly "do his will" by experimenting upon the truths we learn while hearing the word (Step One) and turn our desires to believe (Step Two) into faith-filled action? How do we "give place for a portion" of the word?

This is the role of the patterns we discussed in the previous chapter. When we form spiritual habits, we set in motion a virtuous cycle of righteousness—a series of mutually reinforcing behaviors that perpetuate and magnify positive results. For example, simply attending our church meetings on a regular basis engages us in the ordinance of the sacrament, which commits us to *always* remember the Savior and promises us we will *always* have His spirit with us. Attending our meetings increases our observance of the Sabbath day, which in turn increases our sensitivity to the Spirit. Being at church exposes us to talks and lessons that draw light and truth into our lives and increase our desire to believe. All these things reduce the influence of the adversary and strengthen us to resist temptation.

Now imagine what can happen if we will commit to following additional righteous patterns: temple worship, faithfully serving in our callings, studying and pondering the scriptures, praying with real intent, and otherwise engaging in activities that are "virtuous, lovely, or of good report or praiseworthy" (see Articles of Faith 1:13). Would those patterns not increase the level of spiritual confidence we experience? The answer is self-evident. This is the essence of what it means to experiment on the word.

Step Four: Patiently Nurture Your Faith

Now, we will compare the word unto a seed. Now, if ye give place, that a seed may be planted in your heart, behold, if it be a true seed, or a good seed, if ye do not cast it out by your unbelief, that ye will resist the Spirit of the Lord, behold, it will begin to swell within your breasts; and when you feel these swelling motions, ye will begin to say within yourselves—It must needs be that this is a good seed, or that the word is good, for it beginneth to enlarge my soul; yea, it beginneth to enlighten my understanding, *yea,* it beginneth to be delicious to me. . . . *And behold, as the tree beginneth to grow, ye will say:* Let us nourish it with great care, *that it may get root, that it may grow up, and bring forth fruit unto us.*
(Alma 32:28, 37, emphases added)

In these two scriptures, Alma describes what might be considered the transformation period of our faith. In comparing the word to a seed, He provides a clear image of how we extend the experiment he invited us to take. Once the seed of faith is planted, it must be properly nourished through a belief stage, rather than cast out by impatience and shortsightedness. Like a tender young plant, it is vulnerable and needs diligent care from the gardener.

Faith is nourished by obedience. As we keep the commandments of God, *He* provides the strength we need to continue our experiment (see 1 Nephi 17:3). This is how the *gift* of faith is bestowed. It comes in the form of a power beyond our own that keeps us moving forward. That power is called atoning grace (see Bible Dictionary, "Grace").

Is it that simple? Yes, it is that simple. However, for most, *simple* is easier said than done. Why is that?

We find enduring in faith to be difficult because it is not as immediate as we would like. If we are hungry, we can fix ourselves a sandwich and satisfy our craving in a matter of minutes. In contrast, faith is grown incrementally over an extended period as we demonstrate a *pattern* of obedience in our lives—not just a one-day or week-long exercise. We must show the Lord that obedience is the norm in our life, not the exception—and that kind of commitment requires us to stretch and push ourselves out of entrenched routines.

My experience has been that this kind of commitment is worth making. When we develop an obedience reflex, faith becomes a natural byproduct of the pattern we are living. As a result, when the tests of mortality come, we do not automatically cast the word out and surrender our faith (see Alma 32:28). We recognize the test for what it is and respond by further nurturing our faith. Consider Didi's response in this regard. Faith in Jesus Christ was natural to her because she had nourished its seed through a pattern of obedience and submission to the Lord's will throughout her young life.

Step Five: Acknowledge Your Experience

But behold, as the seed swelleth, and sprouteth, and beginneth to grow, then you must needs say that the seed is good; *for behold it swelleth, and sprouteth, and beginneth to grow.* (Alma 32:30, emphasis added)

Why does Alma tell us that we must acknowledge the growth of the seed? He is not simply making a rhetorical observation. Rather, he is trying to emphasize an expectation the Lord has of us. The Savior reinforced this same principle to Joseph Smith when he said, "Of him unto whom much has been given, much is *required*" (D&C 82:3, emphasis added).

Alma is teaching us that when the Lord provides evidence we are on the right path, and are being led by His light, He expects us to acknowledge the experiment is indeed bearing fruit. The Lord insists we not ignore the fruit and pretend His reassurance was not extended or that direction was not provided. Instead, we "must needs say that the seed is good" (Alma 32:30). This is a requirement that must be fulfilled if we want our faith to continue to grow.

Step Six: Receive a Witness (Knowledge)

And now, behold, because ye have tried the experiment, and planted the seed, and it swelleth and sprouteth, and beginneth to grow, ye must needs know *that the seed is good.* (Alma 32:33, emphasis added)

As Alma continues his explanation of the process of faith, he describes how we should evaluate the evidence our experiment is producing. He tells us how we can "*know* that the seed is good." Through the clear imagery and logic he offers, we learn how belief and faith are transformed into knowledge. Consider how his explanation, below, applies to your ability to address your present challenges and trials.

> And now, behold, *is your knowledge perfect?* Yea, *your knowledge is perfect in that thing, and your faith is dormant; and this because you know*, for ye know that the word hath swelled your souls, and ye also know that it hath sprouted up, that your understanding doth begin to be enlightened, and your mind doth begin to expand.
>
> O then, is not this real? I say unto you, Yea, *because it is light; and whatsoever is light, is good, because it is discernible, therefore ye must know that it is good.* (Alma 32:34–35, emphases added; see also Alma 32:29–35)

Alma's explanation describes what we might call *the goodness test* in the process of faith. If the pattern we are following yields good results (e.g., enlightenment, peace, comfort, greater understanding), then we *know* we are on the right track. If it brings forth bad fruit (e.g., unsettled feelings, animosity, confusion), then we *know* we are headed in the wrong direction.

This is why the previous two steps in the faith process are so critical. If we do not experiment long enough to test our hypothesis, and if we do not acknowledge the evidence the Lord provides that we are on the right track, it will be impossible to subsequently enter the realm of knowing. Our *experience* with the growing seed is evidence it is good and true (see Moroni 7:13–19), hence Alma's comment that because the seed "swelleth and sprouteth, and beginneth to grow, ye must needs *know* that the seed is good" (Alma 32:33, emphasis added).

Notice how Alma transitions from "ye must needs *say*" in Alma 32:30 to "ye must needs *know*" in verse 33, when he describes the evolution of our faith. Experimentation, evidence, recognition, and acknowledgment are the steps that lead to knowledge, and *knowing* allows us to then "press forward with a steadfastness in Christ, having a perfect brightness of *hope*" (2 Nephi 31:20, emphasis added). Is it possible that *saying* the seed is good (Step Five) is the transition point at which the Lord grants us the *knowledge* it is good? I think so.

When we have experimented with faith long enough to experience the things described here, the path to spiritual peace and prosperity becomes clear; therefore, our confidence in pursuing it is increased.

> O then, is not this real? I say unto you, Yea, because it is light; and whatsoever is light, is good, because it is discernible, therefore ye must *know* that it is good. (Alma 32:35, emphasis added)

Step Seven: Endure the Test of Your Faith

For he will give unto the faithful line upon line, precept upon precept; and . . . try you and prove you herewith.
(D&C 98:12, emphasis added)

Sometimes we struggle with the principle of faith because we feel we have applied the process described here and yet our hope in Christ has not been fulfilled as we had anticipated or as we thought we could expect. If we do not understand the trial part of the process, this kind of experience can leave us questioning the principle of faith. It is at this point that some conclude the Lord has abandoned them. As a result, they slide into feelings of despair and hopelessness.

Faith's fulfillment seldom happens when, where, or how we would prefer. The Lord Himself has said, "For my thoughts are not your thoughts, neither are your ways my ways" (Isaiah 55:8). By its very nature, faith requires us to move forward in the face of unanswered questions—trusting in both the direction the Lord is taking us and in His timetable for getting us there. Otherwise, faith would have no role, and our existence on Earth would have no real purpose. For faith to grow, it must be tested.

Elder Lance Wickman, while serving as a member of the Seventy, spoke of this issue in a great address on faith during a general conference. The Lord had chosen to test his faith by bringing home one of his children while still an infant. In his talk, Elder Wickman recounted the events leading up to the death of his son, including the fasts, prayers, and priesthood administrations that were offered in his child's behalf. Certainly, many who exercised faith in behalf of his son wondered why the boy was not spared. Elder Wickman shared this insight about the *why* questions with which we often struggle:

> Do not ever doubt the goodness of God, even if you do not know "why." . . .
>
> In pressing too earnestly for the answer, we may forget that mortality was designed, in a manner of speaking, as the season of unanswered questions. Mortality has a different, more narrowly defined purpose: *It is a proving ground*, a probationary state, *a time to walk by faith*, a time to prepare to meet God (see, for example, Abr. 3:24–25; 2 Ne. 31:15–16, 20; Alma 12:24; Alma 42:4–13) . . . I believe that mortality's supreme test is to face the "why" and then let it go, trusting humbly in the Lord's promise that "all things must come to pass in their time" (D&C 64:32). (Lance B. Wickman, "But if Not," *Ensign*, November 2002, emphases added.)

I experienced an example of Elder Wickman's counsel when, during the week following the passing of Didi's mother, her father said to me, "Bishop, it is not up to God to come to us on *our* terms. It is up to us to go to Him on *His* terms." This simple statement perfectly explains the endurance step of the faith process and gives clarity to Elder Wickman's statement that mortality is largely "the season of unanswered questions."

Although enduring is listed as Step Seven in the faith process, it actually presents itself at each stage in our faith development. Working through difficulties and trials without abandoning patterns of righteousness is part of what it means to nurture faith. If, at the start of our experiment, we understand our faith will be tried and tested, it will be easier for us to recognize the role adversity is playing when it comes our way and why it is so important that we persist in the exercise of our faith.

Step Eight: Renew and Repeat the Process

And now behold, after ye have tasted this light is your knowledge perfect? Behold I say unto you, Nay; *neither must ye lay aside your faith,* for ye have only exercised your faith to plant the seed that ye might try the experiment to know if the seed was good.
(Alma 32:35–36; emphasis added)

Alma makes it clear that the faith process is dynamic, not static. It must be continually renewed until we come to a *fullness* of knowledge and understanding—even perfect knowledge (see D&C 93:12–20, 26–28; D&C 50:24). Our course on faith is not finished until we have completed the work the Lord intends for us in our preparation for exaltation—until we have passed every test and had every experience necessary to purify, sanctify, and ultimately perfect us. And so, throughout our time on Earth—especially during times of temptation, test, and trial—we will need to continually apply the process of faith. Nephi said it this way:

> Wherefore, ye must press forward with a steadfastness in Christ, having a perfect brightness of hope, and a love of God and of all men. Wherefore, if ye shall press forward, feasting upon the word of Christ, and endure to the end, behold, thus saith the Father: Ye shall have eternal life.
>
> And now, behold, my beloved brethren, this is the way; and there is none other way nor name given under heaven whereby man can be saved in the kingdom of God. And now, behold, this is the doctrine of Christ, and the only and true doctrine of the Father, and of the Son, and of the Holy Ghost, which is one God, without end. Amen.
> (2 Nephi 31:20–21)

FOCUS ON THE FRUITS, NOT JUST THE PROCESS

I think our faith journey is best launched by beginning with the end in mind. In other words, our *desire* for greater faith can be kindled by focusing on the *fruits* of faith that have been promised. And what are those fruits? Alma answers:

But if ye will nourish the word, yea, nourish the tree as it beginneth to grow, by your faith *with great diligence, and with patience*, looking forward to the fruit thereof, it shall take root; and behold it shall be a tree springing up unto everlasting life.

And because of *your diligence and your faith and your patience* with the word in nourishing it, that it may take root in you, behold, *by and by ye shall pluck the fruit thereof*, which is most precious, which is sweet above all that is sweet, and which is white above all that is white, yea, and pure above all that is pure; and ye shall feast upon this fruit even until ye are filled, that ye hunger not, neither shall ye thirst.

Then, my brethren, *ye shall reap the rewards of your faith, and your diligence, and patience, and long-suffering*, waiting for the tree to bring forth fruit unto you. (Alma 32:41–43; emphases added)

I find this description of faith's fulfillment to be the clearest and most comforting in all scripture. Following the process that fulfills our faith fuels and feeds our hope of a better world (see Ether 12:4). That hope can motivate us to continually draw upon the "living water" Christ spoke of when visiting with the Samaritan woman at the well (see John 4:10–11). If we will draw from that Source regularly, our desires will become more refined, we will be led to experiment upon the word more frequently, and our faith will be strengthened and then ultimately fulfilled with a knowledge of that thing, whatever *that thing* might be (see Alma 32:34).

CHAPTER 6
Increase Your Obedience

The knowledge which we seek, the answers for which we yearn, and the strength which we desire today to meet the challenges of a complex and changing world can be ours when we willingly obey the Lord's commandments.
(Thomas S. Monson, "Obedience Brings Blessings," Ensign, May 2013.)

KEY UNDERSTANDING 6
Consistent obedience increases our faith, binds the Lord to bless us, and helps us maintain a "brightness of hope" (2 Nephi 31:20).

Daily Life

When I left on my mission, a missionary training center did not yet exist anywhere in the world (the Provo MTC was under construction). Instead, full-time elders and sisters spent three days in a Salt Lake mission home as they entered the field. Those who were going to English-speaking missions went directly to their assigned area from there. However, missionaries who needed to learn a foreign language were sent first to what was then called the Language Training Mission (LTM) in Provo, Utah. My call was to Peru, so at the end of my stay in Salt Lake, the LTM is where I was sent.

Upon arriving at our living quarters in Provo, as the other missionaries and I were getting off the bus, we were greeted by a pair of leaders from the training center. Almost immediately, one of them began reading aloud a list of rules we would be expected to follow during our stay. They included a number of restrictions, such as not being allowed to leave the training facility except to go the bookstore on BYU's campus at designated times, not being permitted to meet up with friends or family members who are in town, not being able to make phone calls, and not being allowed to write letters except on preparation days. I gasped. Somehow, it had never occurred to me that there would be such strict rules while I was still in the states. (Missionaries are much better informed about such matters these days than they were when I entered the field.)

Prior to my mission, I had never been away from my home in California for longer than a week. As a result, I felt homesick before my plane even landed in Salt Lake. In addition, I had been dating a girl I was fond of—whom I had anticipated calling periodically while I was in the LTM. Needless to say, when the rules were delivered, they landed hard.

As the missionary leader finished reading the guidelines and standards, he asked if anyone had any questions. I did not; the rules were clear. All I knew was I did *not* plan to follow them. I distinctly remember saying to myself, *There is no way I'm keeping all those rules!*

However, almost as quickly as my rebelliousness manifested itself, a different thought came into my mind. The Spirit nudged me. *If you are going to do this, you need to do it all the way. Follow the rules and see what happens.* So I did. I kept all the rules.

In pursuit of that standard, I remember disciplining my mind to stay focused all day on the routines we were expected to follow. I made every effort to block out thoughts of home, friends, and family. I learned the discussions. I studied the scriptures. In time, I put away the pictures of my girlfriend I had pinned to the bulletin board in the room where my companions and I slept.

Subsequently, I was asked to serve as the leader of my district. Our entire unit passed off all the discussions in Spanish before leaving for Peru (memorization being the methodology taught at the time). I believe all of this happened because I (along with the other missionaries in my district) had committed to obeying the rules. Too simple a conclusion? I don't think so. This chapter explains why.

Principles

The obedience perspective I gained in the mission field has acted as a template throughout my life. Whenever I have encountered a period of difficulty or begun drifting spiritually, I have returned to the patterns of obedience I learned as a missionary. And each time I have done this, I have experienced a resurgence of spiritual momentum, and my life has improved.

So why has that happened? How is it possible to gain so much power by simply adhering to the commandments? What is the secret?

Well, there is no secret, per se. It is merely how eternal law works. Obedience aligns our lives with the things that bring us to Christ—doctrines and principles and their application. That alignment fuels our faith and expands our hope. As we persist in our steadfastness, we experience the fullness of grace the Savior is willing to grant those who prepare themselves to receive it. Consequently, obedience becomes both a healing balm for and an immunization against fear and despair.

The First Law of Heaven

In the temple, we learn that obedience is the first law of heaven. Having partaken of the forbidden fruit, Adam and Eve were placed under covenant to obey and follow the Lord in righteousness. Knowing this truth should encourage us to nurture obedience as our automatic response when mortality's tests confront us. Consistent obedience is quite literally the *key* to unlocking blessings of peace, comfort, and strength when we are struggling through adversity. However, "because of the simpleness of the way" (1 Nephi 17:41) and our tendency to "[look] beyond the mark" (Jacob 4:14) for solutions to our trials, we often miss this foundational remedy.

As a bishop, I encouraged the youth in my ward to use obedience as their default position in making choices about clothing, entertainment, friends, Sunday sports, dating, and more. I taught them it would always be difficult to know where to draw the line in their conduct if they ignored inspired counsel, instead basing their decisions on the social norms of the day. This, of course, is true for all of us. Making obedience a default position suggests we apply the principle as though it were preprogrammed into our spiritual software when confronted with any choice or when our spiritual reservoir is draining. It becomes our first line of defense against ignorance, sin, remorse, and any other potential failing in our lives. It protects us.

Spiritual power flows to us when we align our actions with the Lord's counsel and commands, because our thinking and behavior are connected to truth, "and whatsoever is truth is light, and whatsoever is light is Spirit, even the Spirit of Jesus Christ" (D&C 84:45). Among other things, this means obedience becomes a conduit to the fruits of that Spirit—love, joy, peace, confidence, spiritual safety, comfort, relief, forgiveness, and more (see Galatians

5:22–25). Those fruits magnify our faith, which in turn fuels an increased desire to obey. And that pattern empowers us to overcome all things.

There is a reason this obedience cycle is so empowering. To understand why, let's explore this principle a little deeper.

The Protection of the Law

The scriptures teach clearly that every blessing we seek and receive from heaven is attached to a corresponding law.

> There is a law, irrevocably decreed in heaven before the foundations of this world, upon which all blessings are predicated—
>
> And when we obtain any blessing from God, *it is by obedience to that law upon which it is predicated.* (D&C 130:20–21; emphasis added)

Taking it one step further, the Lord gives us this promise: "I, the Lord, am bound when ye do what I say; but when ye do not what I say, ye have no promise" (D&C 82:10).

Beyond assuring us that blessings result, Christ made it clear that obedience will also lead to greater joy:

> If ye keep my commandments, *ye shall abide in my love;* even as I have kept my Father's commandments, and abide in his love.
>
> These things have I spoken unto you, that my joy might remain in you, *and that your joy might be full.* (John 15:10–11; emphases added)

Because eternal laws govern the heavens and the earth, our ability to become and remain righteous and joyful is wholly dependent upon our obedience to those laws. Obedience, righteousness, and joy are inseparable from each other (see D&C 121:36). By extension, then, our spiritual momentum depends upon our commitment to learning and complying with the statutes, ordinances, commandments, principles, and doctrines that have been revealed. In the purest of terms, the Lord summarizes His requirement this way: "You shall live by every word that proceedeth forth from the mouth of God" (D&C 84:44). He further clarified the importance of His law to our eternal progress by saying,

> And unto every kingdom is given a law; and unto every law there are certain bounds also and conditions.
> All beings who abide not in those conditions are not justified. (D&C 88:38–39)

Unfortunately, some who hope to find greater capacity to deal with the challenges of life they are facing are not yet fully applying this principle. As a result, they do not find themselves on the right (i.e., correct, beneficial) side of the law. They are at odds with it, and by remaining there, those individuals prevent the heavens from being opened to their view and restrict the Lord from blessing them. In essence, they are placing a barrier between themselves and the healing power of Christ's Atonement by holding at bay the laws that govern its endowments.

The right side of the law is obedience. When we remain obedient to true principles, there is a natural evolution and momentum to the confidence we experience in seeking and obtaining blessings from heaven. Those blessings seem to flow to us consistently and naturally, and our ability to recognize them is unobstructed.

One of the reasons obedience unleashes such an outpouring of blessings is that steadfastness in following the commandments binds the Lord to bless us (see D&C 82:10). God too has to obey—and eternal law requires that when obedience is offered, blessings *must* follow. Our Father simply *cannot* keep them from us, nor does He want to. The law literally prevents Him from doing so. However, just as the Lord is bound to bless us when we keep a commandment, He is equally bound *not* to bless us when we disobey. Why? Because He cannot and will not violate eternal law. It is immutable, and He would cease to be God if He were to act outside its governance (see Alma 42:13; Mormon 9:19).

As a result, those who elect the disobedience side of the law become "a law unto themselves" (Romans 2:14). By making that election, they exclude themselves from the strengthening, enabling, and sanctifying influences of grace (see D&C 88:35). As indicated, the same eternal law that binds the Lord to bless us when we obey prevents Him from doing so when we do not. Accordingly, those who reject or ignore the commandments find themselves at odds with the happiness that obedience and righteousness naturally produce.

Certainly, there are degrees of disobedience. And most do not move from complete obedience one day to the opposite the next. Instead, it happens incrementally. While a few may act out a conscious, open rebellion against God, most engage in a gradual descent from righteousness—one that is sometimes virtually imperceptible while it is occurring. However, regardless of where one falls on the obedience spectrum, keeping the law is the remedy for our spiritual anemia. Yet, because that solution seems too simple, many look for answers in other places (see 1 Nephi 17:41). When they do not find a result they deem suitable, they sometimes curse God and accuse Him of abandoning them when, in fact, the opposite has occurred. *They* have turned away from *Him*. Elder Neil L. Andersen encouraged those so inclined to return to the protective fold of righteousness:

> How do you remain "steadfast and immovable" during a trial of faith? You immerse yourself in the very things that helped build your core of faith: you exercise faith in Christ, you pray, you ponder the scriptures, you repent, you keep the commandments, and you serve others.
>
> When faced with a trial of faith—whatever you do, you don't step away from the Church! Distancing yourself from the kingdom of God during a trial of faith is like leaving the safety of a secure storm cellar just as the tornado comes into view. (Neil L. Andersen, "Trial of Your Faith," *Ensign*, November 2012.)

OBEDIENCE IS THE FOUNDATION OF JOY

In learning and following the law, we lay claim on the eternal joy and peace that our Father experiences. This is because obedience invites light into our being that fills us with Godlike perspective and wisdom. Because knowledge and intelligence flow to those who obey, happiness, confidence, and clarity are among the fruits obedience produces. An enlightened life is a joyful life because it is governed by eternal insight. Here are just a couple of examples of what the scriptures teach in this regard:

———

He that keepeth his commandments receiveth truth and
light, until he is glorified in truth and knoweth all things. . . .

The glory of God is intelligence, or, in other words,
light and truth.

Light and truth forsake that evil one. . . .

And that wicked one cometh and taketh away light and
truth, *through disobedience*, from the children of men, and
because of the tradition of their fathers. (D&C 93:28–39,
emphasis added)

That which is of God is light; and he that receiveth
light, and continueth in God, receiveth more light; and
that light groweth brighter and brighter until the perfect
day. (D&C 50:24)

Is there any question that someone who is filled with light is also filled
with joy? Joseph Smith put it this way: "The Great Parent of the universe
looks upon the whole of the human family with a fatherly care and paternal
regard" (Joseph Smith, in *History of the Church*, 4:595. Used by permission.).
He also said,

He never will institute an ordinance or give a commandment to His people that is not calculated in its nature to
promote that happiness which He has designed, and which
will not end in the greatest amount of good and glory to
those who become the recipients of his law and ordinances.
(Joseph Smith, in *History of the Church*, 5:135. Used by
permission.)

Given this understanding, we can rest assured that the purpose and
design of our Heavenly Father's laws are to bring everlasting joy to our
souls. But beyond obedience's capacity to create a more happy and peaceful
state of being, it is also the mechanism by which we are changed from a
natural man state to becoming like our Father. In that sense, obedience can
be considered an agent of transformation. Elder B. H. Roberts said it this
way:

The man who so walks in the light and wisdom and power of
God, will at the last, by the very force of association, make the
light and wisdom and power of God his own—weaving those
bright rays into a chain divine, linking himself forever to God
and God to him. This [is] the sum of Messiah's mystic words,
"Thou, Father, in me, and I in thee"—beyond this human
greatness cannot achieve. (B. H. Roberts, "Brigham Young: A
Character Sketch," *Improvement Era*, June 1903, 574)

Imagine the power that can come from being linked forever to God
and Him to us. What trial would we not be able to endure? What problem
would we not be able to overcome? What character trait would we not be
able to acquire? What level of peace and comfort would we not be able to
access and sustain?

Given its transformative capacity, obedience should be considered *the*
foundational principle upon which our claim on atoning grace is based.
When we remain true and faithful, even and especially in the face of
adversity and challenge, we create an unbreakable link with our Father
that cannot be severed. By so doing, we make it possible for him to tutor,
magnify, strengthen, justify, and ultimately sanctify us.

Steadfastness in Christ

Overcoming adversity is difficult and can only come about if we have a
compelling vision of something different or better (see chapter 1). Otherwise,
as the initial "hardness" (see 2 Timothy 2:3) of the way manifests itself, we
will waver and search for an easier answer. One of the core premises of this
book is that there is *no* other means to a fullness of happiness and peace but
through Christ and the patterns He prescribes. If we want enduring change
and lasting happiness, we must press forward with faith in *Him* despite our
difficulties. That faith is evidenced by our obedience.

Change through obedience is possible because when we move in the
direction of the Lord, He moves toward us. That is how we will experience
Christ's Atonement. When we obey, the law allows Him to reach down
and carry us through our difficulties. As we apply righteous patterns and
purposes, He quickens and magnifies us. All He asks is that we take those
first few steps. Once we strive to receive *Him* in the world through our
obedience, He will reach down and receive *us* (D&C 84:35–38).

WHAT ENOS LEARNED

And I, Enos, knew that God could not lie; wherefore, my guilt was swept away. And I said: Lord, how is it done? And he said unto me: Because of thy faith in Christ, whom thou hast never before heard nor seen. And many years pass away before he shall manifest himself in the flesh; wherefore, go to, thy faith hath made thee whole. . . . And . . . my faith began to be unshaken in the Lord. (Enos 1:6–11)

WHETHER OR NOT WE HAVE been taught well or have benefited from having family members who provided righteous examples (both of which were true for Enos), at some point each of us must build our own foundation of faith. We cannot rely on the strength and testimony of our parents, the missionaries, Church leaders, or others as we pursue spiritual breakthroughs. This is certainly something Enos seemed to understand and perhaps was one of the things with which he grappled. His record makes it apparent that while he appreciated the things he had been taught, they did not render him immune to spiritual struggle. They were enough, however, to help him know what steps to take when his struggles emerged and how to remain steadfast as he worked through them.

What is interesting to note about the response Enos received at the end of his day-long "wrestle" is that the Lord did not rebuke him for *lacking* faith (something he would later do to Peter, who began to sink after first walking on water). Instead, the Lord told him it was *because* of his faith that he received the resolution he sought (read again Enos 1:8). In other words, Enos's approach to his crisis was evidence of his *trust* in Christ, not proof of an underlying disbelief he harbored. Whatever else Enos was struggling with, he apparently did not doubt the Savior was able to help him.

It defies reason to conclude that the level of faith Enos displayed suddenly emerged on the day he went hunting.

His approach to prayer also suggests such a practice was not something new he was trying out for the first time when he found himself alone in the forest. Instead, all reason tells us that on the day he went hunting, Enos applied principles and practices he had been following for some time. And he followed them because he had faith they would ultimately bring the resolution he sought. If it were otherwise, we would likely read about Enos becoming disaffected and abandoning the things he had been taught. And his record would probably have been even shorter than it is, if we had any record at all.

Each of us should likewise closely examine the foundation upon which we are building and whether the patterns we are following are strengthening or weakening our faith in Christ. What Enos learned was that his persistence and steadfastness were rewarded, not rejected. If we likewise persist in patterns of faith, we too will receive the resolution we seek.

Assessment

To help you determine the extent to which you have endeavored to Build a Strong Foundation (see Principle Two), consider completing this brief assessment. Give each statement a score between 1 and 10 (10 suggesting the statement describes you completely) based on your current state of mind and circumstances. Your scores will help you identify strengths you can build upon and barriers you need to address as you seek to overcome challenges and make spiritual progress.

1. I spend time studying the scriptures every day.
2. I speak to my Heavenly Father in prayer several times a day.
3. I proactively and consistently listen to voices that build my faith in Christ.

4. I have an obedience reflex.
5. I regularly spend my time and means on things that are "virtuous, lovely, or of good report or praiseworthy" (Articles of Faith 1:13).
6. I engage in self-talk that strengthens more than weakens my faith (see the list of contrasting words included in chapter 5).
7. I know how to strengthen my faith when it becomes weak.
8. I am conscious of times when I am disobedient.
9. I view the commandments as blessings that can help me overcome challenges and conquer the imperfect parts of my nature.
10. I hear and obey the promptings that come to me through the Holy Ghost.

As you review your scores, which areas represent strengths you can build upon? Which are areas that could become barriers to your peace if not addressed? List them below.

Strengths to Build Upon:
1.
2.
3.

Potential Barriers to Peace:
1.
2.
3.

Consider making notes about the steps you plan to take to improve your application of this principle.

Actions:
1.
2.
3.

EMBRACE CHANGE

And according to his faith there was a mighty change wrought in his heart . . . *And behold, he preached the word unto your fathers,* and a mighty change was also wrought in their hearts, *and they humbled themselves and put their trust in the true and living God. And behold, they were faithful until the end; therefore they were saved. And now behold, I ask of you, my brethren of the church* . . . Have ye experienced this might change in your hearts?
(Alma 5:12–14; emphases added)

MOST OF US RESIST CHANGE. My sense is this happens because the processes associated with change are usually painful. The concept of a comfort zone describes the desire most of us have to protect ourselves from unexpected or uninvited influences and experiences that might disrupt our world—physically, emotionally, socially, or spiritually.

However, the gospel of Jesus Christ asks us to continually change. The Lord wants us to perpetually pursue a more spiritually refined mindset and higher standards of behavior. In fact, we are commanded to keep changing and progressing "until the perfect day" (D&C 50:24). And certainly, a complete experience with Christ's Atonement is not possible without change.

The *standard* the Lord asks us to apply in considering the changes we need to make is the law as embodied in the new and everlasting covenant of the gospel. That law includes all principles, doctrines, statutes, authorities, keys, ordinances, and covenants taught and practiced in The Church of Jesus Christ of Latter-day Saints. The *instrument* of change, however, is the Atonement of Jesus Christ, without which all men are lost and can neither "act nor . . . be acted upon" (2 Nephi 2:13; see also 2 Nephi 2:21). Through that power, we can alter our course and bring about a change that will allow us to taste the good fruit the gospel promises and have our "newness of life" abide (Romans 6:4).

In this section, we will explore the Lord's prescribed processes of change and how they unlock the atoning grace we rely upon to fulfill the requirements of our mortal probation. Through the

Savior's Atonement, He gained the power to transform us in His image and endow us with confidence about our spiritual state (see 1 John 2:28; Mosiah 27:24–25). As we navigate the tightrope of our imperfections in our daily walk, the Savior's Atonement acts as a safety net to catch us when we fall. It makes it possible for us to get up the next day and try again—because the Savior knew change would need to be a part of our pursuit until we reach "the perfect day" (Proverbs 4:18; D&C 50:24).

CHAPTER 7

Become Clean

We all want progress. But progress means getting nearer to the place where you want to be. And if you have taken a wrong turning, then to go forward does not get you any nearer. If you are on the wrong road, progress means doing an about turn and walking back to the right road; and in that case the man who turns back soonest is the most progressive man. . . . There is nothing progressive about being pigheaded and refusing to admit a mistake . . . Going back is the quickest way on. (C. S. Lewis, Mere Christianity, *www.dacc.edu/assets/pdfs/PCM/merechristianitylewis.pdf, 22.)*

KEY UNDERSTANDING 7

Sincere repentance returns us to a state of innocence before the Lord and empowers us to regain a positive spiritual trajectory in our lives. Because of the Savior's Atonement, we can be washed clean and start our lives anew.

Daily Life

The name of the individual in the following account has been changed to preserve his confidentiality.

It was Stan's third meeting with me as his bishop, and we had been navigating the steps of repentance together. He sat across from me with his head down and just wept. He had fulfilled the assignment I had given him to read *The Miracle of Forgiveness* by President Spencer W. Kimball (Bookcraft, 1969). In doing so, Stan had come face-to-face with the true nature of his sins. That confrontation led him to a level of spiritual anguish he had not experienced before. As a result, his soul ached.

Prior to his recent return to activity in the Church, Stan had been on a journey of self-inflicted torment. He grew up in a difficult home environment; nonetheless, he was exposed to the gospel and taken to church.

He progressed in the Aaronic Priesthood to the office of priest. About that time, he started down a path that far too many find appealing—poor friends, drugs, alcohol, and eventually even gang activity. This led him to also engage in the multitude of transgressions that are byproducts of that lifestyle.

This had been Stan's world for a very long time. However, just prior to coming to see me, he was rescued from the path he was on by a series of miraculous encounters. One of those was a chance meeting on a bus with a member of the Church. Stan shared his story with the member, who subsequently invited him to his home for dinner. The same member encouraged Stan to return to church and schedule time with his bishop, which he did. The inspired advice arrived at just the right moment. Stan had grown weary of the effects of the life he had been leading and had determined he needed to change. But where to begin?

Stan now sat before me in unvarnished openness and humility. No one had manipulated him into being there. He was meeting with his bishop because he wanted to and because he knew he needed dramatic change. One miracle after another had led him to reconsider his ways and to seek help in finding a better path. Now, under the gospel light, his sins came out from under a protective cover of denial and self-justification. They were placed before him in clear view, and the result was a deep pain that comes only to one who fully recognizes that he has been acting at odds with his true identity and eternal nature.

As Stan sat there and wept, I asked him what prompted the tears. "I think I realized before how many people I'd hurt," he said, gathering his composure. "But until now, I don't think I recognized how much I have hurt the Lord, how much I have offended *Him*." This was clearly a turning point for Stan.

Nothing makes the miracle of Christ's Atonement more apparent than to watch it transform the life of a penitent soul. Certainly, that miracle was on display in my meetings with Stan. I watched this once-hardened criminal transform into a man who became sensitive to even the slightest offense he might commit. In the days and weeks that followed this conversation, Stan's agony was replaced by the joy that is promised those who will sincerely repent. Approximately one year after his first meeting with me, Stan was sealed in the temple to a woman he met on his path to a renewed life in the gospel.

Principles

When we distance ourselves from God by violating His commandments, we become spiritually isolated. This sense of separation is exacerbated by the powerlessness we feel to overcome the spiritual pain we are experiencing. And we feel helpless because we do not have the ability to heal spiritual wounds on our own—particularly those that are self-inflicted.

The effect of sin does not dissolve with the passage of time and cannot be remedied by simply avoiding that transgression in the future. Instead, we rely on a cleansing power outside ourselves to restore us to an unspotted state before the Lord and make us spiritually whole again. Only a divinely pre-scribed, Atonement-enabled, grace-empowered solution can accomplish that.

That remedy is called repentance. It derives its cleansing power from the Atonement of Jesus Christ, which was wrought so our sins can be washed away and we can be made clean. This healing gift is available to all who are willing to come to the Lord *on His terms*, with a broken heart and a contrite spirit (see Alma 5:33–34). It is the *only* means of detaching us from the unhappiness and misery that sin imposes and that allows us to lay claim on the fruits of righteousness, which are joy, love, peace, and renewal.

THE EFFECT OF SIN

Simply stated, sin is acting contrary to the laws or nature of God. By violating those laws, we distance ourselves from our Heavenly Father. This, in part, is what creates feelings of guilt and shame. The Light of Christ within us is offended, and our souls become spiritually traumatized. Such trauma teaches us that sin carries consequences that cannot be ignored or wished away. A desire to repent usually occurs once the pain associated with our alienation from God has become so great we would do anything to have it relieved (see Alma 22:15–23).

Since the impact of sin is so injurious, it is certainly something we want to avoid. Yet, the scriptures teach that "all have sinned, and come short of the glory of God" (Romans 3:23). As a result, we should better understand what constitutes sin and how it is committed. It will then be easier to understand how to apply the principle of repentance and to find forgiveness.

As mortals, we commit sins of both *commission* and *omission*. Sins of commission occur when we deliberately violate the commandments. This includes things such as immorality, dishonesty, violation of the Word of Wisdom, criminal activity, acts of cruelty or abuse, and so on.

Sins of omission are more subtle and primarily indicate a kind of spiri-tual negligence on our part. They are the things we *should* do but are not doing because we are holding ourselves back from full engagement in the gospel. They also reflect the self-betrayals we commit when we rationalize and make excuses. Sins of omission include such things as failing to read the scriptures, not praying, withholding praise, not serving with full purpose of heart or pure intent, not expressing gratitude to our Heavenly Father for His blessings, ignoring those in need, and otherwise displaying a measure of complacency in our approach to spiritual matters. James offered a good summary of what constitutes a sin of omission when he said, "To him that knoweth to do good, and doeth it not, to him it is sin" (James 4:17).

When we sin, we place ourselves in a state that is contrary to the nature of God (see Alma 41:11). Because God experiences a perfect fullness of joy, sin brings about an opposite condition (see 2 Nephi 2:11; Mosiah 3:19). Sin keeps us from feeling the happiness God wants us to enjoy and distances us from the ability to experience His love and influence.

Our Father anticipated we would falter in mortality. As a result, He prescribed repentance as the remedy for the spiritual ailment sin would inflict on us. When we sincerely repent, we turn away from darkness and toward light. Repentance is the only way we can bring about a true course correction and unlock the divine forgiveness the Savior's Atonement made possible. Spiritually, it represents the "going back" C. S. Lewis described as necessary for progress to occur when he said, "Going back is the quickest way on" (C. S. Lewis, *The Case for Christianity*, Broadcast Talks in the UK, 1942).

Through repentance, we demonstrate a willingness to humbly acknowledge our sins and seek reconciliation with the Lord. When we do, the Savior forgives us and allows us to move forward with the "newness of life" Paul talked about in Romans 6:4. The desirability of that potential outcome should compel us to engage in the process of repentance *sincerely* and *fully*, holding nothing back.

The Steps of Repentance

Growing up in the Church, I remember being taught the steps of repentance at an early age. However, serving as a bishop deepened my understanding and appreciation of those steps. Each action is critical for anyone who suffers guilt and is seeking greater peace of conscience, and all are essential to unlocking the power and influence of the Savior's Atonement. So let's review them.

Recognition and Acknowledgment

Being humble enough to admit we have sinned is an obvious first step in overcoming our transgressions and turning back, as C. S. Lewis described. Doing so requires a willingness to let go of pride, self-deception, rationalization, or justification and to pursue full reconciliation with our Father in Heaven. It also requires a readiness to *wholly* acknowledge that we have violated His commandments.

As a bishop, it was my experience that some understood this step well enough to feel a measure of guilt when they had transgressed but fell short of a comprehensive understanding of the scope of their sins. Complete repentance requires us to fully recognize, acknowledge, and take responsibility for the breadth of our wrongdoing.

Most of us mature in our understanding of this principle as we grow in knowledge and wisdom over time. Consequently, we may experience periods when a measure of guilt over past sins resurfaces as we more completely recognize the scope of our trespasses. This may or may not mean additional confession to a priesthood leader is required. (If in doubt, meet with your bishop.) Sometimes, it may just mean that a new dimension of our offenses before God has been revealed to us so we can recognize and acknowledge it more fully to our Heavenly Father through prayer.

Godly Sorrow

When repentance is sincere and complete, we experience a significant amount of spiritual pain. The depth of that pain is proportional to the seriousness of our transgressions. This kind of suffering comes naturally when we have a contrite spirit and is a sign that the purging of our sinful nature is underway.

Inner turmoil of this type is called godly sorrow. It is different from feeling embarrassment or even remorse. Godly sorrow is the spiritual dissonance that emerges once we understand how our actions have offended God and distanced us from His Spirit. It is the way we *experience* what it means to die spiritually and should prompt us to acknowledge our unworthy standing before the Lord (see Mosiah 4:11; Ether 3:2). This feeling is what caused Stan to weep while meeting with his bishop after reading *The Miracle of Forgiveness*.

Paul explained godly sorrow this way:

> Now I rejoice, not that ye were made sorry, but that ye sorrowed to repentance: *for ye were made sorry after a godly manner . . .*
>
> *For godly sorrow worketh repentance to salvation not to be repented of:* but the sorrow of the world worketh death.
>
> For behold this selfsame thing, that ye sorrowed after a godly sort, *what carefulness it wrought in you, yea, what*

*clearing of yourselves, yea, what indignation, yea, what fear,
yea, what vehement desire, yea, what zeal, yea, what revenge!*
In all things ye have approved yourselves to be clear in this
matter. (2 Corinthians 7:9–11; emphases added)

The type of sorrow Paul refers to is a critical cleansing agent in our journey back to peace and forgiveness. His declaration is unambiguous. Sorrow "after a godly manner" leads us to want to be fully cleared. The indignation we have is with ourselves. We fear God—at least in the sinful state we are in (see Alma 36:12–19). Our desire and zeal are to obtain a full reconciliation with the Savior on *His* terms, not our own.

There is no substitute for experiencing godly sorrow if we want to fully access the forgiving power of the Savior's Atonement.

Confession

If done sincerely, confession is a step that offers the sinner almost immediate relief. When we confess, we can feel the love of the Savior, and His comfort reassures us that we are pursuing the right course. I am convinced this is one of the Lord's primary purposes for this part of the repentance process. He wants us to have a sense of what His forgiveness feels like so we will more intensely desire to obtain it.

For sins of omission and minor sins of commission, confession to the Lord and the party offended by our actions is adequate. However, more serious sin must include confession to one with priesthood keys who has been designated a "common judge in Israel" (Bible Dictionary, "Bishop"). In a ward or branch, that would be the bishop or branch president.

I have observed at least six outcomes the confession part of the repentance process helps fulfill:

1. Confession shows the Lord we possess the broken heart and contrite spirit required for abiding change to take place.
2. The recognition and acknowledgment steps of repentance are more completely realized during the confession process.
3. An experience with godly sorrow frequently comes most fully as we are confessing our sins.
4. For serious transgressions, the forum of confession allows the bishop (or another "common judge in Israel") to prescribe steps that will help the member make full reconciliation with the Lord.

5. Through confession, the bishop can assess to what extent the Church has been offended or damaged by our misdeeds.
6. The interaction with the Lord's representative allows us to feel a measure of the Savior's love and experience an increase of hope.

Each of these outcomes offers a compelling reason for us to approach confession with full purpose of heart.

The step of confession can be the most humbling part of repentance for some. I am convinced this is one of the reasons the Lord has included it as a necessary step for reclaiming a righteous approach to life. Sufficient humility enables an abiding forsaking of sin to take root.

Restitution

This is a step in our repentance journey that can easily be neglected if we are not careful. Restitution is the process of replacing or repairing what was taken or destroyed because of sins we have committed. The American Heritage dictionary defines it this way:

1. The act of restoring to the rightful owner something that has been taken away, lost, or surrendered.
2. The act of making good or compensating for loss, damage, or injury; indemnification.
3. A return to or restoration of a previous state or position. (The American Heritage® Dictionary of the English Language, Fifth Edition, Boston, MA: Houghton Mifflin Publishing Company, https://ahdictionary.com/word/search.html?q=restitution.)

These definitions offer some perspective about what the Lord expects of us when we have acted contrary to His commandments. When it comes to sin, the issue becomes how and to whom we need to make restitution for what was lost because of our actions. For some transgressions, the path to restitution is obvious. If we have stolen something, we must return the item or pay for it. However, for many sins, the means of restitution can be harder or less obvious to address. For example, if we have engaged in sexual activity outside the bonds of matrimony, how do we restore virtue? If we have borne false witness or engaged in gossip, how do we restore someone's reputation?

There is no such thing as a one-size-fits-all approach or solution to making restitution for sin. Circumstances, sphere of influence, the ability to make contact with the person who was involved in the transgression (or against whom the transgression was committed), and other factors all play a role in how restitution might be correctly addressed. This is one of the reasons it is so important to confess our sins to a priesthood leader with sincerity and complete openness. He can help us determine a course of action that will allow us to make restitution for what was taken and then chart a better course for the future. As we are given instruction about what our acts of restitution should include, it is essential that we follow through completely. We must be willing to do whatever the Lord requires to fully reconcile with Him. There is great mercy in this.

Seeking the Lord's Forgiveness

When we have completed the steps of repentance in sincerity, exercising faith in Jesus Christ, we are justified in asking our Heavenly Father for forgiveness (see Alma 42:13–15). In other words, we have satisfied the demands of justice and can now lay claim on the Savior's mercy. This is a sweet experience for those who have determined they are going to forsake their sins and in whom a mighty change of heart has occurred (see Mosiah 5:2). Asking the Lord for forgiveness is how we *experience* what Christ's Atonement feels like and how we come to know in a personal way that it is real (see Enos 1:4–5).

As with the other steps of repentance, this requires preparation. It should not be handled casually. We need to approach our Father with humility and ask that His tender mercies be extended to us. We must be willing to covenant with him to change and to keep the commandments as we move forward with faith (see Mosiah 5:1–5). We subsequently seal that covenant by partaking of the sacrament with full purpose of heart. Through that ordinance, "the power of godliness is manifest" (D&C 84:20), and we regain a feeling of spiritual wholeness. As we sincerely participate in the emblems of the sacrament, the Lord's healing and forgiving power can be extended to us in a way unattainable through any other means.

Fasting is one of the best ways to demonstrate our humility and contrition as we seek divine forgiveness. This demonstrates meekness and submission as we acknowledge to our Father in prayer that we fell short and acted contrary to His commandments. We can then apologize and ask for His forgiveness with pure intent.

Such a prayer, offered in the name of Jesus Christ, unlocks that part of His Atonement that completes our spiritual healing process. It is a pinnacle moment of reconciliation in which grace works its miracle and we are able to more fully understand what it means to become *at one* with our Savior. It is also the point at which the reason we pray to the Father *in the name of Christ* becomes clearer to us. When we pray in the name of Jesus Christ as part of our repentance, we acknowledge that it is only through His Atonement that we can be reconciled with the Father—which reconciliation we now seek, having done all we were asked to do.

Making a Covenant

Since the purpose of repentance is to initiate permanent and lasting change, making a covenant with our Heavenly Father as we seek His forgiveness is an essential part of the process. Covenants empower us to achieve things in partnership with the Lord that we would not be able to accomplish by relying solely on our own capacities (see chapter 9). The covenants we make as part of the repentance process provide evidence that we are willing to commit to following a path of righteousness and fully turn toward the Savior. In return, He endows us with the spiritual strength we need to persist in righteousness. This is how the enabling power of atoning grace works (see Ether 12:27).

The mathematics of grace in this regard do not follow mortal norms. When we enter into covenants after purging ourselves of sin through the repentance process, our capacity for choosing the right is multiplied, not just added upon. The promises we make in our penitent state first open the door to the Lord's forgiveness and then unlock the power we need to *remain* obedient as we confront temptation. However, if we approach the Lord with something less than a full purpose of heart, we restrict the measure of forgiveness, strength, and peace He is able to give us (see D&C 130:20–21; Moroni 10:4).

Forgiving Self

For many who have committed serious sin, self-forgiveness is the most difficult part of the repentance process. However, what we must understand is that withholding mercy from ourselves after we have sincerely repented is akin to denying the Savior's Atonement. We are essentially rejecting the gift He paid the ultimate price to give us by deeming ourselves unworthy of it. When we do this, we limit the scope of atoning grace and signal to the Lord that we do not consider Him to be the legitimate arbiter of justice and mercy. We put ourselves in that position, and that is not a position we have the right to assume.

When we complete the steps of repentance, we are cleansed of our sins and made spiritually whole. As a result, we have reached the point at which we can and should let go of the self-loathing that commonly accompanies transgression and allow the Savior's mercy to restore our perspective about our divine worth. This step requires us to see things as the Lord sees them and accept that, though we were weak, we can now be made strong (see Ether 12:27).

Once we have acknowledged our sins and repented of them, we have done "all we can do" (2 Nephi 25:23). There are no further actions we can or need to take to save ourselves. Grace is powerful enough to meet the demands of justice and make us eligible for mercy. Forgiveness of self becomes an acknowledgment to the Lord that we accept His Atonement and believe it to have been fulfilled in our behalf. Otherwise, "what doth it profit a man if a gift is bestowed upon him, and he receive not the gift? Behold, he rejoices not in that which is given unto him, neither rejoices in him who is the giver of the gift" (D&C 88:33).

The Promise

Because Jesus Christ took upon *Him* our iniquities, He is able to extend to *us* the promise that our sins will not only be forgiven but forgotten when we repent. And because the Savior's *Atonement* was infinite, His *forgiveness* is equally infinite. It is complete. It is so comprehensive as to render the sin as though it never happened. He said, "Behold, he who has repented of his sins, the same is forgiven, and I, the Lord, remember them no more" (D&C 58:42).

Is It Worth It?

If you have unresolved sin in your life, the repentance process has likely seemed implausible to you. Perhaps embarrassment and fear of being judged have kept you from taking the steps described in this chapter, or you could be worried about hurting someone close to you who is unaware of your past misdeeds. Ultimately, there are many reasons people procrastinate repentance.

So how do you garner the courage and will to begin this process?

I suggest you focus on just two potential outcomes. The first is to consider the promise of peace and healing that accompany repentance. You will be able to reclaim the spiritual identity and confidence that were temporarily masked by transgression and renew your spiritual journey toward exaltation and perfection. You will be let out of the prison cell of guilt and shame that has been holding you hostage and preventing you from experiencing the sunlight of spiritual cleanliness. Think about what it would feel like to experience true joy again in your life.

The second outcome I encourage is to consider the fate of those who do not repent. The Lord has given us a vivid picture of what will happen if we do not address our sins in the way He has prescribed:

> For behold, I, God, have suffered these things for all, that
> they might not suffer if they would repent;
>   But if they would not repent they must suffer even as I;
>   Which suffering caused myself, even God, the greatest
> of all, to tremble because of pain, and to bleed at every pore,
> and to suffer both body and spirit—and would that I might
> not drink the bitter cup, and shrink. (D&C 19:16–18)

Certainly, it is better to be motivated by hope than fear, but I assume the Lord gives us this warning for a reason. He loves us. He loves us so deeply that He took the suffering associated with our sins upon *Himself* so we could escape that burden. It pains Him to think we might have to *unnecessarily* experience the pain He already endured in our behalf.

Few promises from the Lord are more reassuring than this one: "Come now, and let us reason together, saith the Lord: though your sins be as scarlet, they shall be as white as snow; though they be red like crimson, they shall be as wool." (Isaiah 1:18)

I hope you will allow such an assurance to guide your next steps toward repentance.

CHAPTER 8
Make Regular Course Corrections

Each one of us has been given the power to change his or her life. As part of the Lord's great plan of happiness, we have individual agency to make decisions. We can decide to do better and to be better. In some ways all of us need to change; that is, some of us need to be more kind at home, less selfish, better listeners, and more considerate in the way we treat others. Some of us have habits that need to be changed, habits that harm us and others around us. Sometimes we may need a jolt to propel us into changing. (James E. Faust, "The Power to Change," Ensign, November 2007.)

> KEY UNDERSTANDING 8
> We experience atoning grace in greater measure when we humbly heed inspired correction and routinely realign our behavior with standards of righteousness.

Daily Life

The Christmas season is an especially busy time for a bishop. Holiday planning and events get layered on top of the regular church administrative meetings, ward business, and interviews that already occupy so much of his time. Throughout the holidays, unforeseen crises still occur, and people who are experiencing economic hardship need an extra measure of focus and care. And then there is tithing settlement, which usually occupies a good portion of multiple Sundays as well as several weeknights. In addition, when I served as bishop, in December our stake put on two events for the community that we were asked to support as missionary and public affairs opportunities. In short, at Christmastime there is no scarcity of time demands on a bishop.

Because of that, I was not particularly excited during one holiday season when our stake president asked the bishops to attend a meeting with our area authority and the California Carlsbad mission president on the Sunday before Christmas. The meeting was scheduled for 12:30 p.m. at a chapel in a neighboring stake. Its purpose was to introduce us to *Preach My Gospel*, which was just being rolled out throughout the Church.

That year, our sacrament meeting ran from 11:00 a.m. to 12:10 p.m. As a result, I anticipated heading over to the bishop's council right after our service. I figured leaving right after the closing prayer would get me to the other building by about 12:25, just prior to the start of the meeting.

As often occurs, our Christmas program ran long that day. To compound the problem, I was on the agenda to offer concluding remarks. *Oh well*, I thought. *Certainly, being late to the missionary meeting will be forgiven under the circumstances.* I arrived at the other building about ten minutes late and joined the bishops meeting in progress.

Unfortunately, I was not the only one who was tardy. Consequently, at the close of the meeting, our stake president asked us to linger so one of the bishops (who had been on time) could fill the rest of us in on what we had missed. It was apparent our leader was not pleased with the lack of respect our actions represented.

The day after the meeting, I sent an email to our stake president apologizing for my tardiness and explaining my circumstance. I anticipated a response something like, *No problem; I understand.* Instead, this was his reply:

> *Bad form. There were only three bishops there at the start of the meeting. One didn't bother to show up at all. It was embarrassing. You should plan ahead and make arrangements so you can be to such meetings on time.*

Needless to say, the response stung. To add to my embarrassment, all the bishops were copied on his reply (presumably so others who were late or absent would get the same message). *Really?* I thought. *I deserve this?*

As the rebuke sank in, however, I loosened my hold on my pride and allowed for a bit more self-reflection. I realized this wise leader was giving me correction that was both needed and deserved. This was not an isolated incident. I was late to meetings too often. It was a bad pattern. In addition, our stake president had frequently counseled the bishops of our stake about the importance of being on time. "If you are not ten minutes early to a meeting, you are late," he would say with a smile. In short, he should not have had to reiterate guidance he had already given me. He had previously taught me (and others) what was expected. These thoughts tempered my feelings and perspective.

After a few minutes of personal evaluation, I realized the appropriate response to my leader's email was to accept the correction I had just been given and learn from it. As a result, I sent an apologetic reply indicating I knew better and therefore should have done better. I asked for the email addresses of our area authority and the mission president so I could likewise apologize to them, which I subsequently did. I also sent a message to the other bishops communicating my regret for how my tardiness had affected them.

Pain absorbed. Problem acknowledged. Lesson learned. Course correction begun.

Principles

It may seem to you that the rebuke I received in this situation was a bit harsh. If so, I doubt you think the incident merited any kind of deep cleansing, as we discussed in the previous chapter, on my part. After all, I was simply late to a meeting, right?

While I appreciate that benevolent view, it obscures a critical principle we must all learn and master. Although my tardiness to a meeting was not a deliberate act of disobedience or rebellion, it *was* evidence that I had a bad habit that needed to be confronted and fixed. The stake president was calling attention to something in my behavior that needed to change. And my *feelings* about his response did not alter the truth he revealed. There were things I was doing that were inconsistent with what the Lord expected of me. And as a loving priesthood leader, he cared enough about me to let me know.

Elder D. Todd Christofferson explained the principle this way:

> Consecration therefore means repentance. Stubbornness, rebellion, and rationalization must be abandoned, and in their place submission, *a desire for correction, and acceptance of all that the Lord may require.* This is what King Benjamin called putting off the natural man, yielding to the enticings of the Holy Spirit, and becoming "a saint through the atonement of Christ the Lord" (Mosiah 3:19). (D. Todd Christofferson, "Reflections on a Consecrated Life," *Ensign,* November 2010, emphasis added)

All of us must learn to receive correction with a spirit of acceptance if we want to experience Christ's Atonement more fully in our lives. Criticism, such as the kind I received from my stake president, is usually hard to hear. None of us enjoys learning we have fallen short. But if we will accept the feedback and give it sincere consideration, it can be a channel to betterment and eventual spiritual wholeness. Because unless our deficiencies are confronted and addressed, we run the risk of preventing the enabling power of Christ's grace to help us overcome obstacles and accelerate our growth.

The reality is sometimes we *invite* difficulty into our lives. This happens when we slacken our adherence to the patterns of righteousness we discussed earlier, leaving us vulnerable to temptation. That vulnerability often prompts us to make choices that place us on a downward trajectory, spiritually and emotionally. This state can then lead us to make decisions that *lessen* our ability to find healing and relief at the very time we need *increased* peace and a clearer perspective.

In short, as we become casual with our spiritual habits, we distance ourselves from God and the help and healing He wants to provide. We compound that gap when we avoid self-reflection or reject inspired counsel. Here is why that matters.

Imagine what might have happened to me spiritually had I chosen to remain offended by my stake president's justified rebuke. What if I had initiated an angry exchange with him in that moment? At a minimum, it would have created a strained relationship. On a more serious level, it could have caused me to speak ill of him around others and poisoned both his reputation and mine—not to mention put fellow saints in spiritual jeopardy. Think of all the potential disastrous ripples of that scenario playing itself out.

Because there are potential long-term implications of our *daily* responses to mortality's difficulties, we must adopt repentance as a continual agent of change and recalibration in our lives. It is not a practice we engage in only when we have committed serious transgression. It is the way we remain perpetually immersed in an experience with Christ's Atonement.

Through the humility that attends sincere, ongoing self-examination, we invite grace to remain active within us. That power multiplies our ability to improve, change, and handle adversity with strength, humility, and dignity (see Ether 12:27). Additionally, it increases our desire and ability to resist temptation and to sustain a more hopeful perspective. Ultimately, grace helps us conquer the things that weaken our character and rise above the misery and despair that so often disable us (see Principle Five).

INITIATE CHANGE EARLY ON

The probation aspect of mortality is relentless; it never sleeps. As a result, it is critical that we engage in the practice of checking ourselves often and then making course corrections immediately and with adequate resolve if we find ourselves diverging even slightly from what the scriptures refer to as the "narrow" way (2 Nephi 9:41; see also Alma 34:32–34). The reason this is important is because Satan is a brilliant strategist. He knows he has only to persuade us to dabble in the spirit of rebellion or self-pity to eventually weaken our character and prevent us from reaching our celestial destination (see D&C 10:5–7, 20, 22–27).

Satan does not usually attempt to persuade righteous people to come out in open rebellion against God. He knows that kind of temptation would easily be rejected. Instead, he looks for opportunities to take advantage of our vulnerabilities when we are discouraged and worn-out. Because the adversary's approach is so subtle, we often fail to recognize when we are inviting him to have influence over us. We invite his influence by *allowing* anger, discouragement, offense, hurt, rebellion, and other negative responses to mortality's tests to take root. We also do so by weakening our standards or engaging in sins of omission—irregular prayer, intermittent church attendance, neglecting scripture study, not participating in service opportunities, and so on. Once we let our guard down, we open ourselves to choices that will lead us further away from an experience with atoning grace. That downward spiral usually occurs like this:

1. We slacken our commitment to patterns of righteousness because we are going through a difficult time—or, conversely, we do not feel the need for consistent spiritual nourishment because things are going so well. In either case, our spiritual immune system is weakened.
2. In our vulnerable state, we entertain sinful behavior—something we would previously have easily rejected—and begin looking for excuses to act on it.
3. Eventually (and inevitably), we act on that urge and rationalize it to be no big deal. We also seek out like-minded people who affirm, "Oh, everybody does *that*" or "It's justified, given what you're going through."
4. The action we take provides a degree of immediate relief or pleasure, albeit temporary. Because it offers some respite, we desire more, so the action is repeated a second, then a third time.

5. To dull the spiritual pain these actions create, we begin an offensive against our conscience. We do this by trying to drown it out through further engagement in sinful practices, adding to the ones we have already committed.

6. In time, our new behavior becomes a habit. And if the behavior involves the use of numbing substances (e.g., alcohol, drugs), that habit usually morphs into an addiction.

7. Habits and addictions subsequently alter our character and mask our true spiritual identity. This is because the Light of Christ within us has been dimmed and our spiritual sight has become impaired.

8. Once a new character is formed, our new desires and habits gain full control. We then begin to define ourselves by these new behaviors.

9. Now this new character that has been built on patterns of *un*righteousness leads us to not only reject goodness but to embrace sin.

10. At this point, what began as a misguided attempt to find a measure of comfort and peace has become a cycle of misery and outright opposition to righteousness (see Mosiah 2:36–37).

The deeper we allow that spiritual descent to go, the more difficult it becomes to exercise faith and hope that our lives can improve—and the harder it will be to repent and alter our course. Regrettably, this is when some decide there is no point in even living anymore or they determine they cannot change or be forgiven. To protect ourselves from this kind of spiritual decline, we must learn to recalibrate our thoughts and actions at the first sign we have relaxed our standards or departed from the essential patterns of righteousness we discussed in chapter 4.

As we apply the principle of repentance comprehensively, sincerely, and early on, we are able to recognize the correct path more readily and have confidence about where we are headed. Through the humility that attends sincere, ongoing self-examination, we invite grace to remain active within us. In turn, that power magnifies our ability to improve, change, and handle adversity with both strength and meekness (see Ether 12:27). Additionally, as we receive that enabling power, our desire and ability to resist temptation increases. We are given the strength to overcome the things that weaken our character. That is what an experience with Christ's Atonement promises.

RECONCILIATION

The Lord's term for the ongoing spiritual alignment we have been discussing is *reconciliation* (see 2 Nephi 10:24; 33:9). To reconcile with someone means to square any differences and become more unified. When we reconcile with another person, the issue that caused the separation is resolved, and the previous *whole* we once enjoyed is restored, even strengthened.

In a spiritual or eternal context, when we engage in repentance as a means of ongoing reconciliation, we create greater alignment with our Redeemer, which fulfills the purpose of His Atonement by placing us *at one* with God (see Bible Dictionary, "Atonement"). As a result, *continual* reconciliation with the Savior should be our primary concern and focus during mortality. Such a squaring through *daily* repentance is the way we acknowledge our complete dependence upon Christ's atoning sacrifice and exhibit our willingness to do anything to be right with Him. *Right*eousness, then, becomes the fruit of reconciliation. It is the state we achieve when what we do is approved by the Lord, having our sins remitted and being made clean through our ongoing repentance (see Ether 12:37).

We need the rescuing power of the Savior's Atonement to be *continually* in full force in our lives. If we form the habit of making course corrections early on, the Lord's rescuing power will likewise be extended early on—and then abide.

CHAPTER 9

Make and Keep Covenants

Now, to each member of the Church I say: keep on the covenant path. Your commitment to follow the Savior by making covenants with Him and then keeping those covenants will open the door to every spiritual blessing and privilege available to men, women, and children everywhere.
(Russell M. Nelson, *"As We Go Forward Together,"* Ensign, April 2018.)

KEY UNDERSTANDING 9
Engaging in a covenant relationship with God magnifies our ability to bring about enduring change and have an abiding experience with atoning grace.

Daily Life

During a gospel doctrine class one Sunday, our teacher had us read together these verses from the Book of Mormon:

> And now it came to pass that when the king had made an end of these sayings, and all the people were assembled together, they took their swords, and all the weapons which were used for the shedding of man's blood, and they did bury them up deep in the earth.
>
> And this they did, it being in their view a testimony to God, and also to men, that they never would use weapons again for the shedding of man's blood; and this they did, *vouching and covenanting with God, that rather than shed the blood of their brethren they would give up their own lives . . .*
>
> And thus we see that, when these Lamanites were brought to believe and to know the truth, they were firm, and would

suffer even unto death rather than commit sin; and thus we
see that they buried their weapons of peace, or they buried the
weapons of war, for peace. (Alma 24:17–19, emphasis added)

At the conclusion of our reading, the teacher asked, "What are some
ways making covenants can strengthen our ability to make changes in our
lives, as it did for the Lamanites?"

After several class members offered ideas, a mother of four young children timidly raised her hand. When called upon, she shared this experience
and insight:

> For a long time, I struggled with getting angry at my children.
> I knew it wasn't the way the Lord wanted me to respond to
> them, and I always felt bad when I lost my temper. But no
> matter how hard I tried to do better, my frustrations seemed
> to control me. So I decided to make a covenant with God
> to be more patient. Since that time, I can't say that I've been
> perfect, but just making that covenant has made me more
> mindful of my anger and helped me seek better ways to
> respond when I feel stressed. (From author's personal notes)

Principles

This mother viewed making covenants as a powerful tool that could
help her affect lasting change in her life. Because of her struggle, she was
willing to make a sacred promise with her Heavenly Father to do better. By
doing so, she acknowledged her weakness and communicated a need for
God's help to become more Christlike in her parenting. She was essentially
putting this pledge from the Savior to the test:

> And if men come unto me I will show unto them their weak-
> ness. I give unto men weakness that they may be humble;
> *and my grace is sufficient for all men that humble themselves*
> *before me*; for if they humble themselves before me, and have
> faith in me, then will I make weak things become strong
> unto them. (Ether 12:27; emphasis added)

Anyone who wishes to improve the trajectory of their lives must learn how
to apply this same principle. Note the Lord's instruction about how and when

His grace becomes sufficient for us to overcome our struggles and the parts of the natural man with which we all wrestle: it is when we humble ourselves before Him. That's it? Yes, that's it. When we are humble, we can access His grace, which *is* sufficient to make weak things become strong unto us.

The experience of the young mother in the Sunday School class teaches us that making covenants evidences to God that we have become sufficiently humble to receive the Savior's grace. It is a way of saying, "Father, I am struggling. I can't do this on my own. I need Thy help. I promise to do all I can to overcome this challenge. I pray my humility is sufficient for Thee to grant me the strength to do better and be better." By covenanting with our Heavenly Father, we make ourselves eligible for the help only He can provide, which enables us to make changes that endure. This enabling power is available because of the Savior's Atonement, without which the sufficiency of grace would not exist and our ability to rise above our current spiritual, emotional, or physical state would be impossible.

BECOMING SPIRITUALLY SELF-SUFFICIENT

The Lord wants us to be able to overcome opposition and effect change in an enduring way. For that to happen, He must empower us to become more like Him (see 3 Nephi 12:48). Therefore, His aim is to transfer *His* power to *us*, thereby granting us the ability to triumph over adversity and temptation, not just sometimes but always. He knows that once we begin operating through the power He has granted us, our perspective will be more enlightened, we will be less impatient with our circumstances, and our trust in His purposes and timing will increase. As a result, we will begin to view and deal with our mortal experience in a more faith-filled and hope-oriented manner. More importantly, we will be able to overcome the tests mortality relentlessly offers.

Covenants make it possible for us to develop and enjoy the fruits of this kind of spiritual self-reliance. This may feel almost counterintuitive since, by their very nature, covenants *bind* us to the Lord. Being bound would seem to imply greater instead of less dependence on Him. However, expressing our need for divine help is an act of spiritual maturity that draws atoning grace into our lives. That power increases and sustains our ability to meet the demands of our second estate in an enduring way.

When we consistently keep our covenants, our characters are transformed. Once that happens, we are no longer just *trying* to be more Christlike. We actually *become* men and women of Christ with a fully formed capacity to overcome all things, just as He did (see D&C 75:16). In other words, His power replaces our own when we make ourselves eligible for the endowment of grace He has promised to give us.

In this way, keeping covenants changes the Savior's Atonement from an abstract doctrine into a real power that strengthens and sustains us every day throughout our mortal journey. As a result, we should deepen our understanding of what it means to make and keep sacred covenants.

The Meaning and Purpose of Covenants

In their simplest form, covenants are tools of improvement. The Lord uses them to help us become purer, more charitable, and more Christlike but also more resilient, courageous, and spiritually committed. They are sacred promises made between God and us. When we *make* a covenant, we commit to God that we will act in a certain way and conform to the standards He prescribes. As a result, covenants require us to set aside *our* interests and agenda and adopt *His*. The Lord's promise is that by doing so, we will receive the blessings that will most benefit us.

By making sacred promises with the Lord, we commit to approach life in a more elevated and edifying way. We acknowledge to God our need for change and that we cannot accomplish it without His help. Sometimes that recognition comes when we have been worn down by the deadening experience of sin. Other times, that recognition grows out of our desire to overcome a weakness or to rise above a challenge. In all cases, real, abiding change can be accomplished only by partnering with the Savior. And we engage in that partnership by making and keeping covenants with our Heavenly Father.

Unlike secular contracts, the covenants we make with God are entered with someone who is both the Source of Light and Truth and the Author of Salvation. He is a person of perfect integrity, omniscient perspective, and omnipotent capabilities. As such, we can be assured that He will never violate His part of the agreement and is fully able to fulfill His promises. It is *our* faith and obedience that are tested through the covenant relationship. Elder Henry B. Eyring explained it this way:

> The Latter-day Saints are a covenant people. From the day of baptism through the spiritual milestones of our lives, we make promises with God and He makes promises with us.

He always keeps His promises offered through His authorized servants, but it is the crucial test of our lives to see if
we will make and keep our covenants with Him. (Henry
B. Eyring, "Witnesses for God," *Ensign*, November 1996.)

The perspective Elder Eyring offers is important because if we adopt the
idea that the Lord has something to prove, we might approach making covenants as a kind of negotiation. When we carry this kind of mindset into
making covenants, we tend to approach our Heavenly Father with a precon-
ceived idea of what His response should be to the promises we make. In other
words, we imply we expect a certain result in exchange for holding up our
end of the agreement, and when the outcome we want is not forthcoming,
we think God failed to live up to His part of the bargain. For example, we
may say something like this: "If you will help me get this job, I promise I will
always be a full tithe payer" or "Lord, I am a full tithe payer, so can you please
grant me this career opportunity?" These expressions are certainly innocent
enough and no doubt reflect a sincere desire. And I am not suggesting our
Father is offended by them, per se. But do you see the spirit of negotiation in
those statements? We seem to be implying that if we are *not* granted the job
or career opportunity we are seeking, we will no longer be full tithe payers.
I mean, that was the agreement, right? So we are setting conditions on our
willingness to obey, albeit inadvertently. We are essentially telling the Lord
what blessings we believe we should receive as a result of the commitments
we are making.

Our frame of mind is critical in this regard because it determines whether
our faith will be strengthened or weakened through the covenant process.
Too often, we fail to recognize the fulfillment of the Lord's promises because
we have imposed expectations on the Lord that are inconsistent with the
spirit of making covenants. We misunderstand our place in the covenant
relationship.

Contrast that approach with the response Shadrach, Meshach, and
Abed-nego had when confronted with a magistrate who insisted they serve
his gods or be placed in a fiery furnace:

Shadrach, Meshach, and Abed-nego, answered and said to
the king, O Nebuchadnezzar, we are not careful to answer
thee in this matter.

If it be so, our God whom we serve is able to deliver us from the burning fiery furnace, and he will deliver us out of thine hand, O king.

But if not, be it known unto thee, O king, that *we will not serve thy gods, nor worship the golden image which thou hast set up.* (Daniel 3:16–18, emphases added)

Note how the three Israelites expressed full faith that the Lord could (and, in fact, would) deliver them from a fiery fate. Yet, their obedience was not conditioned on whether or not He did. They would refuse to serve the king's gods regardless of the outcome. They manifested a deep trust and foreknowledge that whatever happened was a reflection of the mind and will of the Lord and would be consecrated for their gain (see 2 Nephi 2:1–3). They understood their role in the covenant relationship was to keep their promises and trust in the Lord, come what may.

In the end, Shadrach, Meshach, and Abed-nego *were* delivered from the effects of the fiery furnace, and the Lord was seen in their midst as they stood unaffected by the flames (see Daniel 3:24–25). Is it possible that the three Israelites' willingness to keep their covenants on the Lord's terms (and not their own) produced the faith necessary to draw the Lord into their presence and save them? Is it conceivable that it was their complete trust in the Lord that produced the outcome they sought? I think so, and here is why.

The covenant the three friends had made with God was to be obedient and to trust Him. They did not place a condition on the Lord as to how their obedience should be rewarded. They had faith that God would know what was best for them in the context of the broader purposes He needed to fulfill.

This no-strings-attached approach to their obedience was rewarded with the gift of faith. As a result, at a crisis moment, they were confident the Lord would deliver them. However, they needed the king to know that whether their interpretation of deliverance meant being saved from death or had more eternal implications, they would still keep their covenants. What is not stated in the record, but is implied by the friends' response to the king's threat, is that Shadrach, Meshach, and Abed-nego trusted the Lord's promises would be fulfilled in their behalf regardless of any immediate consequences they suffered: "But if not . . . we will not serve thy gods, nor worship the golden image which thou hast set up" (Daniel 3:18). The Lord's promise was to endow them with faith sufficient to make their trust in Him unwavering. Such a gift is the greatest assurance the Lord can offer for His part in the covenant relationship. In fact, regarding those who receive the gift of faith as a result of keeping their covenants, He said this: "Ye shall say unto this mountain, Remove hence to yonder place; and it shall remove; and nothing shall be impossible unto you" (Matthew 17:20).

I once heard a business leader who is a member of the Church say it this way:

> The Lord doesn't *depend* on any of us to accomplish his work, but we can reach a point where He can *count* on us—He can trust us. When that happens, the laws of gravity no longer apply. (From author's personal notes)

When we approach covenant making with the Lord in the manner demonstrated by Shadrach, Meshach, and Abed-nego, we develop greater confidence that the Lord will fulfill His promises. And when we keep our part of the covenant, we earn His trust in us. That combination (our confidence in the Lord and His trust in us) produces the faith we need to navigate the challenges and opportunities of mortality. While we may not literally move a mountain or defy gravity, we will possess God's limitless power in accomplishing His purposes concerning us. And as Mary was told upon learning she would be the mother of the Son of God, "With God nothing shall be impossible" (Luke 1:37).

Two Types of Covenants

Because covenants play such an important role in our spiritual development, it is important that we have a correct understanding of their nature and what it means to keep them. Broadly speaking, there are two types of covenants, and both are necessary. Combined, they help us successfully meet the tests of mortality and make us worthy of a celestial life.

Covenants Associated with Ordinances

We make one type of covenant when we participate in saving ordinances prescribed by the Lord. These include baptism, confirmation, priesthood ordination, and temple ordinances. (The sacrament is an extension and renewal of our baptismal covenant.) Ordinances are physical, outward performances we engage in that represent internal, spiritual commitments we make. They are sacred rituals that make clear the commitments and promises we pledge to keep.

The Lord has reserved His most far-reaching blessings for those who enter into and keep the covenants associated with His saving ordinances. When we receive them with a sincere heart and real intent, God's power is more fully manifest in our lives (see D&C 84:20–21). Among other things, this means we are granted the ability to be healed, lifted, strengthened, cleansed, renewed, and sanctified. This is because faithfulness to our covenants unlocks the door to a more complete endowment of the Savior's grace.

Ordinances and covenants derive their transforming power from the Atonement of Jesus Christ. Without that act, ordinances would have no saving power, and covenants would be meaningless, because there would be no means of redeeming us from either death or our corrupted state (see 2 Nephi 9:7–9). We would be lost forever, so covenants and ordinances would have no significance. However, because He fulfilled and finished His mission, the Savior possesses the power to make us spiritually complete—even perfect—through the saving ordinances we receive and the associated covenants we keep (see Moroni 10:32–33).

Personal Covenants

The other type of covenants we engage in are personal in nature. These are the individual commitments and promises we make to God that are specific to our circumstances, mortal capabilities, and weaknesses. For example, we might make a covenant to listen to others more empathically or to arrive on time to our meetings. We could covenant to be more consistent or thoughtful in our prayers or more diligent in our temple attendance. However, even these kinds of covenants draw their power from the ones we enter into when receiving saving ordinances (see D&C 84:20–21). They become specific representations of the more generalized commitments we make through baptism, confirmation, priesthood ordination, and our temple endowment.

For example, the young mother who promised the Lord she would be a more patient parent extended and personalized the covenant she made at baptism to stand as a witness (and example) of God "at all times and in all things, and in all places that [she] may be in" (Mosiah 18:9). Similarly, a young man who covenants to accept a mission call manifests a willingness to put the oath and covenant of the priesthood into real-life practice (see D&C 84:33–48). In each case, the Lord rewards acts of committed discipleship with an outpouring of power to help His children *keep* their covenants.

WHAT IT MEANS TO KEEP OUR COVENANTS

The case made so far is that ordinances and covenants draw magnificent blessings into our lives if we keep them. So what exactly does that mean? How do we *keep* our covenants?

The Lord has given us some clues about how that question might be answered. One of them was this revelation to the Prophet Joseph Smith:

> And I now give unto you a commandment to beware concerning yourselves, to give diligent heed to the words of eternal life.
>
> For thou shalt live by every word that proceedeth forth from the mouth of God. (D&C 84:43–44)

This instruction implies that there are things about our nature that we need to guard against ("beware concerning yourselves"). And to conquer them, we must live by *all* of God's words. Because *all* can seem a bit overwhelming, perhaps it would help to break the term down a bit and discuss what "live by every word" might mean. Let's divide this standard into four steps or parts:

1. *Seek* the word.
2. *Receive* the word.
3. *Remember* the word.
4. *Live* according to the word.

Seek

Seeking the word implies we make a proactive effort to learn and understand what the Lord expects of us (see D&C 58:26–29; 107:99–100). Sincere seekers reject the notion that ignorance is bliss. Those who truly desire to keep their covenants commit to "seek the face of the Lord always" (D&C 101:38), knowing that by searching out the Lord's will and committing to follow it, He will manifest Himself to them more clearly and fully (see D&C 93:1).

Seeking also implies real intent on our part. Seeking is not just curiosity. It is wanting to know because we intend to act—and wanting to act because we desire to become like Him with whom we engage, through the covenants we make (see Moroni 10:4–5; Moroni 7:48).

Receive

The principle of receiving speaks to our attitude toward the word once we have heard it. Those who receive the word in faith with a predisposition to obey will hear, then act. This is what it means to "heed" or "hearken" to the word (see D&C 84:43–47). *Receiving* the word suggests the word prompts us to change and improve. And when we truly receive the word, we embrace that idea.

The scriptures teach us that *the word* is synonymous with light and spirit and truth (see D&C 84:45). As such, it is communicated through channels of revelation. So if we want to receive the word, we must learn what those channels are and how they function. By extension, we must also learn how to receive revelation.

The Lord uses two channels to reveal His word to us: the priesthood channel and the personal channel. While each is distinct, we need both to fully receive the word. These channels work together to give us a more complete understanding of truth. So let's define them, shall we?

The priesthood channel refers to revelations that are given through those who hold keys within the kingdom or those acting under their direction and authority. General conference is an obvious example of the word coming to us through priesthood channels. While general conference teachings have application to all members of the Church, when we are prayerfully seeking to *receive* the word, we will often feel as though those messages were intended for us personally—as though the Lord is speaking directly to us through His servants. In fact, He is. The two channels of revelation work together in this way. In the Lord's economy, He can speak to the many and the one at the same time.

Personal revelation is direct inspiration and instruction we receive from our Heavenly Father through the power and influence of the Holy Ghost. We initiate it by engaging in deep and intimate communication with our Father through prayer. His response can come in a variety of ways. It may come through a conversation we have with a friend or family member or in a talk someone gives in sacrament meeting or general conference, as mentioned above. A series of events or encounters may make it clear that the Lord is communicating something to us. Often, direct revelation will occur as we are immersed in the scriptures, where most of the answers to our spiritual yearnings and questions can be found (hence, the importance of *seeking* the word). Regardless of the means through which the communication occurs, we will need the Spirit in order to recognize and understand what the Lord is telling us. The Spirit can especially help us if we are consistently inviting His guidance in our patterns of study.

Regardless of the channel through which revelation comes, to fully receive the word, we must hear it and then act with diligence on the instruction we have been given. When we combine hearing with doing, we are keeping our covenants.

Remember

To keep our covenants, we must also live in remembrance of the promises we have made with the Lord. Among other things, this implies we treat our covenant responsibilities as stewardships for which we consider ourselves accountable (see D&C 107:99–100). Those stewardships include our callings, our roles in our families, our priesthood or Relief Society duties, temple and missionary work, and the intimate, personal assignments we receive from the Holy Ghost. This is not to suggest we will do any of these things perfectly. However, part of remembering our covenants is to recognize and acknowledge when we err and reconcile quickly and early on with the Lord regarding our shortcomings (see chapter 8).

The reason we engage in some ordinances regularly is so that we will, in fact, remember. For example, we participate in the sacrament weekly so we can be reminded that the Savior should be the focus of our remembrance. Through that ordinance, we renew the covenant we made at baptism to take His name upon us. As we partake of the emblems of his flesh and blood, we covenant to "always remember Him" (D&C 20:77, 79). That weekly renewal allows the Savior, who is the Source of the word, to fill us with eternal perspective and magnify our desires for righteousness. Such desires will lead us to remember.

In his fervent exhortation to his sons Nephi and Lehi, Helaman summarized the principle and purpose of remembrance perfectly:

> And now, my sons, *remember, remember* that it is upon the rock of our Redeemer, who is Christ, the Son of God, that ye must build your foundation; that when the devil shall send forth his mighty winds, yea, his shafts in the whirlwind, yea, when all his hail and his mighty storm shall beat upon you, it shall have no power over you to drag you down to the gulf of misery and endless wo, because of the

rock upon which ye are built, which is a sure foundation,
a foundation whereon if men build they cannot fall.
(Helaman 5:12, emphasis added)

Live

It has been my observation and experience that if we sincerely seek, receive, and remember the word, *living* it comes pretty naturally. A pattern of seeking, receiving, and remembering changes our desires and compels us to live according to the word. In fact, to do otherwise would create a spiritual dissonance that would plague us until we aligned our behavior with what the word is telling us we should do. The internal disharmony we experience when we *do not* act in accordance with the covenants we have made is one of the ways the Holy Ghost prompts us to get back on the path the Lord has prescribed. In that respect, *not* following through once we have sought and received the word is more difficult than acting on our covenants, because spiritual unrest is painful.

Living according to the word unlocks the full power of the Savior's atoning grace (see Psalms 119:16). Grace comes to us as we do all within our power to fulfill the promises we have made (see 2 Nephi 25:23). Doing all we can do simply means we try our best to understand and apply the word we have sought and received. As we live our lives this way, we demonstrate to the Lord that we do, in fact, remember.

Now, we should not anticipate that we can apply these principles intermittently or independent of each other and expect to achieve meaningful change. Instead, we should treat them as interdependent, each needing to be practiced consistently and continually. When we view them as parts of one covenant-keeping whole, seeking, receiving, remembering, and living act as spiritual connective tissue that maintains the health of our soul. Consequently, they are principles that need to be applied over and over again throughout our lives.

THAT SAID . . .

Spiritual progress is incremental. We do not effect lasting change in a week, a year, or even a decade. It is a lifelong pursuit and will continue after we die. As such, we should view covenants as tools that can help us make steady progress one day and one principle at a time. None of us will master all there is to seek, receive, remember, and live at once. Such mastery will require patience, which is why the Lord offers us His grace—to empower us each step of the way as we persist in our pursuit of perfection.

Those who keep their covenants learn that an obligation to the Lord is an opportunity to lay claim on the Atonement of Jesus Christ and draw upon the infinite yet personal power it bestows. As soon as we accept the obligations associated with making covenants, the Savior transfers *our* burdens to *Him*. And by *keeping* our covenants, we make Him a partner in our spiritual development and progress. That partnership makes failure impossible and success inevitable.

WHAT ENOS LEARNED

And I will tell you of the wrestle which I had before God, before I received a remission of my sins.
(Enos 1:2)

IT IS APPARENT FROM ENOS'S record that when he went to "hunt beasts in the forests" (Enos 1:3), he knew his standing with the Lord was not all it should be. At least, it was not all he *wanted* it to be. One does not "wrestle . . . before God" because he feels everything is spiritually calibrated in his life. Clearly, Enos felt something needed to be reconciled.

That said, in his account he does not tell us the exact nature of his struggle. Instead, he focuses on the action his spiritual hunger prompted him to take and what happened to him in response. His experience parallels that of Joseph Smith, who likewise sought to know if his sins had been forgiven and approached God directly, in search of His approval. Both men received an answer, and their lives were never the same as a result.

What we observe in Enos is someone who was honest enough with himself to recognize he needed a course correction and that he alone was responsible for taking remedial action. He did not blame his parents, disavow doctrine, or rail against God about his dilemma. Rather, his actions demonstrated a willingness to "follow the Son, with full purpose of heart, acting no hypocrisy and no deception before God, but with real intent," as his uncle Nephi had taught (see 2 Nephi 31:13).

Not only does Enos not reveal what he was concerned about the day he went hunting, he also does not tell us what he spoke to the Lord about all day in prayer. We do not know what weaknesses he discussed, sins he confessed, promises he made, or questions he asked. He simply tells us that the starting point of his experience was a wrestle before God, and the ending point was having his "guilt . . . swept away" (Enos 1:6). It seems Enos wanted us to focus on the most critical thing he learned from his experience. When change is needed, we must confront it. Ignoring the need for change will just compound our suffering. And if we seek to reconcile ourselves with the Lord, He will hear and help us. We can trust Him.

What Enos learned is that spiritual progress is stunted when we allow something unresolved to stand between us and the Lord. And that impediment can be removed only through honest soul-searching and ongoing repentance. Few messages could be more important for us to hear.

ASSESSMENT

To help you determine the extent to which you "Embrace Change" (Principle Three), consider completing this brief assessment. Give each statement a score between 1 and 10 (10 suggesting the statement describes you completely) based on your current state of mind and circumstances. Your scores will help you identify strengths you can build upon and barriers you need to address as you seek to overcome challenges and make spiritual progress.

1. I have the desire and the will to overcome my sins.
2. I have experienced the peace that full repentance offers.
3. I believe the Lord will forgive and forget my sins if I sincerely repent.
4. I recognize when I need to make course corrections in my life.
5. I am aware when I am being tempted by the adversary.
6. I talk to the Lord about my weaknesses and ask Him to give me the strength to overcome them (see Ether 12:27).
7. I make personal covenants with the Lord about the things I need to change.
8. I have received all the saving ordinances and covenants for which I am eligible at this stage of my life.
9. I honor my covenants, and they influence the choices I make.
10. I consistently seek, receive, remember, and live the word.

As you review your scores, which areas represent strengths you can build upon? Which are areas that could become potential barriers to your peace if not addressed?

Strengths to Build Upon:
1.
2.
3.

Potential Barriers to Peace:
1.
2.
3.

Consider making notes about the steps you plan to take to improve your application of this principle.

Actions:
  1.
  2.
  3.

FILL YOUR LIFE WITH LIGHT

Now, this was what Ammon desired, for he knew that king Lamoni was under the power of God; he knew that the dark veil of unbelief was being cast away from his mind, and the light which did light up his mind, which was the light of the glory of God, which was a marvelous light of his goodness—yea, this light had infused such joy into his soul, the cloud of darkness having been dispelled, and that the light of everlasting life was lit up in his soul, yea, he knew that this had overcome his natural frame, and he was carried away in God. (Alma 19:6)

DARKNESS IS NOT A GOOD place to linger for any length of time. Whether it be emotionally, spiritually, or physically induced, darkness invites fear, despair, worry, and hopelessness. In all its forms, darkness is the playground of the adversary, who wants us to lose faith and surrender our hopes and aspirations. His aim is to make us "miserable like unto himself" (2 Nephi 2:27). As a result, when we remain mired in a state of guilt, anxiety, despondency, or anguish, we are allowing the prince of darkness to have influence over us (see Joseph Smith Translation, John 14:30).

If we find ourselves trapped in this state of mind, the solution is to draw more light into our lives. The scriptures teach that "God is light, and in him is no darkness at all" (1 John 1:5). To help us understand the power of light, the Lord offers this insight:

> That which is of God is light; and *he that receiveth light, and continueth in God, receiveth more light*; and that light groweth brighter and brighter until the perfect day.
> And again, verily I say unto you, and I say it that you may know the truth, *that you may chase darkness from among you.* (D&C 50:24–25, emphases added)

The ability to reject darkness and embrace light is essential to having an experience with Christ's Atonement. In fact, the presence of light is how that experience is manifest. When we receive relief, enlightenment, insight, perspective, strength, or peace, our lives are filled with light. As a result, the effect of atoning grace is clear to us.

When we routinely and systematically draw light into our lives, darkness can have no power over us. This is why righteous patterns are so critical. They ensure we constantly draw on sources of light and prevent Satan's designs from having any lasting impact. Such was the insight Nephi gained when he was given an interpretation of his father's dream about the rod of iron and the tree of life. Note how he described the river of filthy water his father saw and Lehi's response to it:

> And I said unto them that the water which my father saw was filthiness; and *so much was his mind swallowed up in other things that he beheld not the filthiness of the water.*
> (1 Nephi 15:27, emphasis added)

Lehi was neither drawn to nor distracted by the "filthiness of the water," because his mind was focused on holier things. His preoccupation with light literally prevented him from seeing the filthiness of the water. It was not a matter of Lehi denying there was darkness. Rather, the darkness had no effect on him because he was focused on activities and thoughts that nourished his spirit and allowed him to partake of the fruit of the tree of life (see 1 Nephi 8:10–12).

To rise above the temptations and trials that mortality imposes, we must be like Lehi. We must fill our lives with holiness and reject darkness. We should seek to have our minds "swallowed up in other things" so we cannot see "the filthiness of the water"—so darkness cannot influence us. In the section that follows, we will examine the things we can do to be governed by light and protected from the darkness Satan tries to impose on us.

CHAPTER 10
Examine Your Heart

Individual agency is so sacred that Heavenly Father will never force the human heart, even with all His infinite power. Man may try to do so, but God does not. To put it another way, God allows us to be the guardians, or the gatekeepers, of our own hearts. We must, of our own free will, open our hearts to the Spirit, for He will not force Himself upon us.
(Gerald N. Lund, "Opening Our Hearts," Ensign, May 2008).

KEY UNDERSTANDING 10
We can only experience Christ's Atonement and the strengthening power of His grace if our hearts remain soft and open. And because of agency, we alone determine whether light or darkness will influence us.

Daily Life

Most people who knew my mother thought she was a saint. And they are right to feel that way. She truly embodied the qualities of charity as well as anyone could. However, even those who knew her well are likely unaware of the depth of her goodness. Here is what I mean.

Mom could have become a very different person had she allowed a difficult upbringing to negatively influence her outlook on life. Instead, she made a choice not to let her childhood prevent her from experiencing joy and a hope-filled view of life. She kept her heart open to what the Lord was trying to teach her through the things she was asked to endure.

Mom was born in New York City to a mother who had some fairly significant health problems. Her own father left the family when she was about four years old, and she never saw him again. She heard from him only once after that, receiving a postcard from him on her seventh birthday. She was raised by her grandmother, an aunt, and to a lesser extent, her mother.

As she grew up, Mom received little information about her father, and the things she was told about him were largely negative. She knew nothing of his whereabouts. She was in her sixties before she was finally able to make contact with some members of her father's family who were able to fill in some of the blanks for her about him. Among other things, she learned her father had wanted to see her but was prevented from doing so by the women who had raised her.

Despite the circumstances of her upbringing and its aftermath, Mom chose not to be bitter. Instead, she exercised a healthy curiosity about what caused her father to leave and withheld judgment about his decision. That curiosity led her to consider his circumstances: he had married a woman who had grand mal epilepsy, which he was unaware of until his new bride had a seizure on their wedding night, and his mother-in-law and his wife's aunt had taken control of the care of his only child, among other pressures. Mom felt a measure of compassion for him. That compassion protected her heart from anger and kept it open to forgiveness.

Because she deliberately nurtured a softened heart, I do not remember ever hearing my mother speak ill of her father or complain about her childhood. When she talked about either, she always communicated a sense of understanding and offered context and perspective. It seems she did not want her children to grow up with a negative impression of their grandfather or think that she should be pitied because she did not have a relationship with her dad. She protected her father's reputation and never conveyed any sense of victimhood about her upbringing.

After Mom passed away, my siblings and I spent time going through her journals. Reading her entries gave us further insight into the principles that guided her and how she acquired such a pure heart. The phrase she used more than any other in her writings was, *I feel so blessed*. We ultimately had those words engraved on her headstone. Our mother found the gospel when she was thirty-six and considered it to be the greatest gift she had ever received. In her records, there were multiple expressions of gratitude for her husband, who joined the Church two years after she did, her four children, and her grandchildren. She wondered what she had done to deserve such blessings.

After Mom died, my sister gave a letter to my two brothers and me that our mother had written many years prior. She wanted her husband and children to have it after she passed away. It was written when she was still in a healthy state, physically and mentally (both of which deteriorated later in life). This is that letter.

April, 1988

Dear George and family,

As I write this I am of sound mind (most of the time) and body, and it is my constant prayer that our Father in Heaven may see fit to allow me to serve out my allotted time on earth being able to be useful and active. Most of all I pray I may not become a burden to anyone.

As I read and hear of people my age who have been deprived of their ability to function on their own, I get concerned for the welfare of my family in the event I join that group somewhere down the road.

Should a time come when I need your support and strength, I hope it will be of short duration—I will appreciate your caring about me—hopefully not for me. I do not want to complicate your lives in any way.

I hope you will be able to remember the good times—and know how much I appreciate my husband and family—and the privilege I've had of getting to know the wonderful spirits sent to all of us. I must have done something right to be so blessed.

The greatest gift I could ever give to any of you is the gift of acceptance of the gospel—paving the way for all of us to be members of His church with all the blessings it holds.

I have a strong testimony of the power of prayer and know it has brought each of us through many a crisis or rough spot. I want you each to know that I have spent much time on my knees for you as you have reached crossroads in your life, and always my prayers have been answered.

I pray you will continue to use this great gift of prayer—and do all you can to strengthen your own faith.

I love you all very much.

Annette

Mom

I hope the words my mom expressed in her letter give you a sense for the light that so completely permeated her heart. Once she was introduced to the gospel, it became *the* guiding force in her life. Her involvement in the Church and dedication to her family filled her with love and gratitude. As she grew older, her life was no freer from trials and challenges than it was in her childhood. However, whenever adversity struck, instead of feeling sorry for herself, Mom would always ask God what she was supposed to learn from the experience. She would not allow darkness in. She chose to seek greater light.

Principles

Certainly, I do not mean to suggest that my mom was perfect, and she would likely be embarrassed by what I have written about her here. But there is a point to what I share about her example of a charitable life. What we learn from my mother's story and how she chose to deal with a difficult upbringing is that none of us are victims in mortality. We can control how we respond to our circumstances (see 2 Nephi 2:26–28). We can *choose* to rise above adversity. We achieve this frame of mind and strength of spirit, at least in part, by paying attention to the condition of our hearts and seizing command of the attitude we adopt toward our mortal condition.

When God sent us to earth, he endowed us with the gift of choice—agency. This means we alone determine what our thoughts and the intents of our hearts will be. In other words, agency makes us responsible for shaping the attitude we will adopt toward both the good and bad experiences we have during this earthly journey. This means we *choose* whether light or darkness will influence our frame of mind when things do not turn out as we hoped or expected.

My Mom chose light, and for this I am grateful.

Often, as we anticipate and experience the demands of our second estate, we become discouraged and even despair. However, even though our Father has put us fully in charge of our response to life's tests on Earth, He did not leave us alone to face the opposition that makes agency possible (see 2 Nephi 2:11). He gave us a Redeemer—a *Savior*. As a result, through the power of His Son's Atonement, *we* can gain the power to conquer darkness; it does not need to enter and then remain in our lives. Because Christ's grace is real, we can lay claim on a force that will literally cover our weakness and grant us an enduring capacity to choose righteousness over sin and despair, as well as light over darkness, in every earthly circumstance (see 2 Nephi 2:26–28).

Because this is true, our ability to rise above our condition is a function of what is happening *within* us. It is not determined by external forces or influences. We decide if our hearts will be open or closed, softened or hardened. As such, we must be willing to honestly confront our pride, eliminate self-deception, and let go of all human tendencies that impede our spiritual growth, because until we fully yield our hearts to Christ, we keep Him at arm's length. When we keep Christ at a distance, grace remains a dormant, untapped power (see Mosiah 3:19; Helaman 3:35).

With that in mind, let's explore why the heart plays such an important role in our quest to have an experience with Christ's Atonement and what we can do to prepare it for greater openness and purity.

THE CONDITION OF OUR HEARTS

The scriptures teach that the heart is one of the primary portals through which the spirit communicates. It is a gatekeeper that determines the amount of eternal communication we will allow ourselves to receive. It is also *the* key channel upon which we depend to hear those things that will help us address and overcome mortality's tests and unleash our spiritual progress.

The Book of Mormon often uses the term *heart* to describe the attitude we exhibit toward Heavenly Father's teachings and the overall state of our spirits. For example, those who are proud and unwilling to change are commonly referred to as hard of heart (see Alma 12:10). In contrast, the same record also uses the term *heart* in sharing examples of humble saints who set aside their pride, such as those who "yield[ed] their *hearts* unto God" (Helaman 3:35, emphasis added). King Benjamin preached that those who want to gain access not only to the knowledge of heaven but to the qualities and attributes of God must become "as a child, submissive, meek, humble, patient, full of love, willing to submit to all things which the Lord seeth fit to inflict upon him, even as a child doth submit to his father" (Mosiah 3:19). Each of those adjectives describes the condition of one's heart, spiritually speaking. Through numerous accounts, the Book of Mormon makes clear that our heart plays a central role in the amount of light and darkness we permit to govern us.

Our hearts, then, either allow the Holy Ghost to influence us or prevent Him from doing so. In our mortal condition, our senses, instincts, emotions, and intellect often rule our spirits. When allowed free reign, they create a condition of heart that is prideful and hardened. In contrast, when we surrender to the Holy Ghost's promptings and direction, the Savior empowers us to transform even adversity into opportunities for our spiritual refinement and progress so we do not become embittered by those challenges. This is why my mother's heart remained unhardened. She invited the Holy Ghost's influence and allowed it to change her.

If we want to be yoked with Christ, who is the Source of Light, as we face life's challenges, we must first grant Him access. We must open the gate that guards our heart and proactively invite the right spirit to take up residence there. This begins by our listening to the right *voices*, as we discussed in chapter 4. Here is how the Lord explained this principle to Hyrum Smith: "Put your trust in that Spirit which leadeth to do good—yea, to do justly, to walk humbly, to judge righteously; and this is my Spirit" (D&C 11:12).

Moroni furthers our understanding of "that Spirit" with this insight:

For behold, the Spirit of Christ is given to every man, that he may know good from evil; wherefore, I show unto you the way to judge; for every thing which inviteth to do good, and to persuade to believe in Christ, is sent forth by the power and gift of Christ; wherefore ye may know with a perfect knowledge it is of God. (Moroni 7:16)

As indicated, because we alone determine the amount of light or darkness that will be allowed to influence us, it is important we each consistently examine the condition of our heart. The Lord's instruction in Doctrine and Covenants 11:12 and Moroni 7:16 gives us some clear criteria for that examination. Using these verses as our guide, perhaps we should consistently ask ourselves: "What am I feeling 'led' or 'persuaded' to do by my present attitude and frame of mind?" An honest answer to that question will help us quickly assess whether we are inviting light or darkness into our hearts. Taking it one step further, we might ask ourselves these two questions at the end of each day to assess how well we are following Moroni's counsel: "In what way was Christ *revealed* by my actions and choices today? In what way was He *concealed* by my actions and choices?

Hardening Our Hearts

The opposite of an open and receptive heart is a hardened heart. This describes those whose attitudes toward righteousness have become darkened by resisting the Holy Ghost, instead surrendering to the influence of the adversary. Our hearts typically harden little by little over time as we allow spiritual insensitivity and callousness to take root. Once we give those tendencies control, it becomes more difficult for us to *feel* what is right and what is wrong (see 1 Nephi 17:45). And *feelings* are experienced in the heart.

Our hearts increase in openness to "that Spirit which leadeth [us] to do good" (D&C 11:12) as we pursue righteousness in earnest. Conversely, a hard heart is the byproduct of abandoning the spiritual habits that protect and preserve our spiritual well-being. Alma described this correlation in clear terms:

It is given unto many to know the mysteries of God; nevertheless they are laid under a strict command that they shall not impart only according to the portion of his word which he doth grant unto the children of men, *according to the heed and diligence which they give unto him.*

And therefore, *he that will harden his heart, the same receiveth the lesser portion of the word*; and he that will not harden his heart, to him is given the greater portion of the word, until it is given unto him to know the mysteries of God until he know them in full.

And they that will harden their hearts, to them is given the lesser portion of the word until they know nothing concerning his mysteries; and then they are taken captive by the devil, and led by his will down to destruction. (Alma 12:9–11, emphases added)

Why is receiving the "lesser portion of the word" so spiritually damaging? And what exactly is the "word" to which Alma refers? The Lord answered that question in this instruction to Joseph Smith: "For the *word of the Lord is truth*, and whatsoever is *truth is light*, and whatsoever is *light is Spirit, even the Spirit of Jesus Christ*" (D&C 84:45, emphases added). He further explained:

And truth is knowledge of things as they are, and as they were, and as they are to come. . . .

The Spirit of truth is of God. I am the Spirit of truth. . . .

He that keepeth his commandments receiveth truth and light, until he is glorified in truth and knoweth all things. (D&C 93:24–28)

These verses teach that the "word" is synonymous with truth, spirit, and light. Therefore, when we allow our hearts to become hardened, we close ourselves off from an *enlightened* view of life and our circumstances. We develop a kind of spiritual blindness that prevents us from seeing "things as they are, as they were, and as they are to come" (D&C 93:24), which is the very definition of truth that the word represents and teaches. This perspective impairment leads to further thoughts, choices, and patterns of behavior that fill our souls with darkness (see chapter 8). Alma says that those who follow such a path "are taken captive by the devil, and led by his will down to destruction" (Alma 12:11). Certainly, being under Satan's destructive control is a very dark place to be.

This principle makes clear the importance of the righteous patterns discussed earlier in this book. It also explains why we must make corrections early on if we find ourselves drifting from the gospel path and how critical it is that we repent continually. These righteous patterns are the means the Lord has given us to prevent the downward spiral Alma described.

An Inability to Forgive

There are many ways we can develop a hardened heart, thereby inviting greater darkness into our lives. One of the most common is an unwillingness to forgive. While this tendency manifests itself in different forms, the outcome is the same: darkness takes root because we allow guile to overwhelm charity in our response to an offense. Once we open the door to that kind of darkness, the hurt and pain we experience starts to fester. That darkness begins to affect other parts of our character and nature. It leads us to become bitter, and we start treating ourselves as victims, justifying our attitudes because of the wrongs committed against us. This frame of mind can ultimately impact the relationships we have with people not even involved with the offense, such as family members, friends, work associates, or fellow Saints. Most importantly, it can impact our relationship with the Savior, who is full of light and can heal us.

It is impossible to identify all the potential offenses we might experience as we interact with fellow mortals; they can range from the trivial to the profound. However, regardless of their origin or depth, the Lord has made clear what our response to them must be:

> Wherefore, I say unto you, that ye ought to forgive one another; for he that forgiveth not his brother his trespasses standeth condemned before the Lord; for there remaineth in him the greater sin.
>
> I, the Lord, will forgive whom I will forgive, but of you it is required to forgive all men.
>
> And ye ought to say in your hearts—let God judge between me and thee, and reward thee according to thy deeds. (D&C 64:9–11)

For many, this commandment is a hard pill to swallow. *Certainly*, some are tempted to think, *the Lord didn't mean* this *situation when He commanded us to forgive* all *men*. And it is easy to have compassion for those who feel this way. Innocents have suffered deeply because of injustices committed against them. For them, forgiveness can understandably seem too much to ask. Yet, the Lord did not qualify His commandment or offer exceptions.

If an inability to forgive is the source of a hardened heart, there are two truths that can help us. The first is that we have a Savior who is filled with mercy and love. He performed His atoning mission so the demands of justice could be reconciled and ultimately appeased. Because His sole desire is to bless us and fill us with joy, we can know that the design and purpose of every commandment He gives us is to increase our happiness and remove burdens we carry. Therefore, by commanding us to forgive, He is showing us the pathway to peace. His aim is to lighten our load, not make it heavier.

The second truth that can help us overcome an inability to forgive is that the Savior does not give us any commandment that is beyond our ability to keep (see 1 Nephi 3:17). He will *always* show us a way to fulfill what He has asked us to do—and grant us the strength to conquer the obstacles that stand in the way of our complete obedience (see D&C 95:1). In every circumstance we might encounter, He can point to an instance in His own life that stands as an example of how we should respond. More important, His Atonement unleashed the power of grace, which enables us to overcome that which seems impossible to overcome. As a result, we do not have to deal with our offenses alone. The Savior stands ready to help us and will ultimately "wipe away all tears from [our] eyes" (Revelation 21:4).

Most of us struggle with the commandment to forgive because of an innate allegiance we feel to justice. We reject unfairness almost instinctively and reason that if we extend forgiveness, our offender will never learn his lesson or be brought to account for his deeds. We believe that extending mercy is an affront to fairness and allows the perpetrator to essentially get away with it. We rationalize that withholding mercy is justified because the person who caused us pain has not yet *earned* our forgiveness.

This thought process evidences a misunderstanding of the laws of justice and mercy and how they apply to the seemingly unforgivable acts we may be called upon to endure. First of all, the Lord has never suggested that those who commit offenses—whether small or large—will go unpunished for their transgressions. In fact, He has said quite the opposite. The Lord has consistently emphasized that He will hold the unrepentant accountable for their actions. Here are just two scriptural examples of many that could be given:

> I, Jacob, would speak unto you that are pure in heart. Look unto God with firmness of mind, and pray unto him with exceeding faith, and he will console you in your afflictions,

and he will plead your cause, *and send down justice upon those who seek your destruction.* (Jacob 3:1, emphasis added)

And "Leave judgment alone with me, for it is mine *and I will repay.* Peace be with you; my blessings continue with you" (D&C 82:23, emphasis added).

If we have been a target of abuse, or otherwise the victim of another person's actions, no amount of justice we attempt to impose on our offender will heal us from the pain that results, nor should we think acts of punishment or retribution we might engage in are somehow worthy substitutes for the justice the Savior will exact on unrepentant souls. He alone has a perfect understanding of the measures of justice and mercy that should be meted out and what the timing of each should be.

Before we can achieve a state of peace in the wake of offenses, we must first accept that seeking justice and withholding forgiveness will never lead to the spiritual or emotional recovery we need. In fact, such behaviors will have the opposite effect. Acting on our feelings of anger and bitterness keeps us from experiencing the mercy that can heal us and to which we are entitled.

Justice and mercy are often thought of as opposing principles when, in reality, they are companions. They work in harmony, and each needs the other for the plan of redemption to be effectual (see 2 Nephi 2:11; Alma 42:15–25). For example, when abuse is the issue, the Lord will pour out justice upon the abuser unless that person repents (see Alma 42:16–18). God's justice will cause that person to suffer far beyond anything we could impose by withholding forgiveness. Consider this description of the suffering the Lord says the unrepentant will experience: "how sore you know not, how exquisite you know not, yea, how hard to bear you know not" (D&C 19:15).

Moreover, if we are the recipients of someone's offense, we have a claim on mercy. Mercy frees us from the pain abuse causes and replaces bitterness with peace. However, to access the Lord's mercy, we must first extend forgiveness. That is why the Lord commands us to forgive. He wants us to experience the comfort only He can provide, and He wants us to be restored to a state of joy. Elder Lynn G. Robbins explained it this way:

> In this scenario of the abused wife, we have two parties—the abusive husband and the victim-wife, both of whom need

divine help. Alma teaches us that the Savior suffered for both: for the sins of the man and for the anguish, heartache, and pain of the woman (see Alma 7:11–12; Luke 4:18).

To access the Savior's grace and the healing power of His Atonement, the Savior requires something from both of them.

The husband's key to access the Lord's grace is *repentance*. If the husband doesn't repent, he cannot be forgiven by the Lord (see D&C 19:15–17).

The wife's key to access the Lord's grace and then allow Him to heal her is *forgiveness*. Until the wife is able to forgive, she is choosing to suffer the anguish and pain that He has already suffered on her behalf. By not forgiving, she unwittingly denies His mercy and healing. In a sense, she fulfills this scripture:

I, God, have suffered these things . . . that they might not suffer . . .

But if they would not repent [or forgive,] they must suffer even as I.

(D&C 19:16–17) (Lynn G. Robbins, "Be 100 Percent Responsible," *BYU Speeches*, August 2017, emphases added.)

Through His commandment to forgive, the Lord is, in effect, offering this admonition and invitation to us regarding the offenses we experience: "Let me handle this. That person is accountable to me, not you, for justice. You can let go of the burden of trying to exact justice yourself. Your job is to extend forgiveness. If you can do that, I will heal your feelings of violation, hurt, pain, and bitterness. That was the purpose of my Atonement and is the power of my grace."

Because of the Savior's propitiation, He alone is able to determine how and under what circumstances justice and mercy will be extended. He is also the only one entitled to make those judgments. Similarly, only He is able to bind up our wounds (see Luke 10:34) and heal us of our infirmities. A personal pursuit of justice cannot accomplish that for us.

As a result, our focus should be *solely* on reconciling with *Christ* and exercising trust in *His* mercy and justice. As Nephi counseled,

Reconcile yourselves to the will of God, and not to the will of
the devil and the flesh; and remember, after ye are reconciled
unto God, that *it is only in and through the grace of God that
ye are saved [or healed]*. (2 Nephi 10:24, emphases added)

Helping us overcome our inability to forgive is one of the ways Christ's
Atonement exhibits its personalized influence. It is both infinite and
intimate enough to free us from the darkness that hardens our hearts and
replace it with an abundance of light (e.g., healing, recovery, relief, peace).
Elder Dale G. Renlund offers a fitting summary in this regard:

Whether we suffer because of troubled relationships, economic challenges, or illnesses or as a consequence of someone else's sins, *the Savior's infinite Atonement can heal even—
and perhaps especially—those who have innocently suffered.* He
understands perfectly what it is like to suffer innocently as
a consequence of another's transgression. As prophesied, the
Savior will "bind up the brokenhearted, . . . give . . . beauty
for ashes, the oil of joy for mourning, [and] the garment of
praise for the spirit of heaviness. (Dale G. Renlund, "Latter-
day Saints Keep on Trying," *Ensign*, May 2015, emphasis
added.)

Whether the darkness we experience stems from a lack of forgiveness
or some other issue, the solution is the same: we must yield our hearts to
God. This begins by our demonstrating a willingness to seek and do our
Heavenly Father's will and to align our desires with His. We accomplish
this by following the patterns spoken of in chapter 4. As we engrain those
practices into our lives, our Savior fills us with His light. That spirit of
willingness changes any disposition we have to invite darkness into our
hearts and replaces it with an increased desire to seek more light and act
charitably (see Mosiah 5:2).

CHAPTER 11

*Re*learn How to Pray

Prayer is a supernal gift of our Father in Heaven to every soul. Think of it: the absolute Supreme Being, the most all-knowing, all-seeing, all-powerful personage, encourages you and me, as insignificant as we are, to converse with Him as our Father. Actually, because He knows how desperately we need His guidance, He commands, "Thou shalt pray vocally as well as in thy heart; yea, before the world as well as in secret, in public as well as in private."
(Richard G. Scott, "The Supernal Gift of Prayer," Ensign, *May 2007.)*

> KEY UNDERSTANDING 11
> When we sincerely apply the correct tenets of prayer, we accelerate and deepen our experience with the Savior's Atonement.

Daily Life

Sitting in the congregation during a sacrament meeting in 2001, I was touched by a song performed by a young sister in our ward. I suppose I had heard the hymn "Where Can I Turn for Peace?" before, but when it was sung that day, it was as though I was hearing it for the first time. It felt like the soloist was preaching a sermon on prayer and I was her only audience.

The lyrics of the hymn affirm that prayer offers us the opportunity to experience the Atonement in an immediate and personal way as we seek to overcome challenges and trials. The words were particularly significant to me because of some things that were happening in my life at that time. They also reflected my personal experience with prayer.

Where can I turn for peace?
Where is my solace
When other sources cease to make me whole?
When with a wounded heart, anger, or malice,
I draw myself apart,
Searching my soul?

Where, when my aching grows,
Where, when I languish,
Where, in my need to know, where can I run?
Where is the quiet hand to calm my anguish?
Who, who can understand?
He, only One.

He answers privately,
Reaches my reaching
In my Gethsemane, Savior and Friend.
Gentle the peace he finds for my beseeching.
Constant he is and kind,
Love without end.
("Where Can I Turn for Peace?" *Hymns*, no. 129)

Principles

Prayer is about as ubiquitous a topic as can be found in the Church, is it
not? You and I would be hard-pressed to sit through our Sunday meetings
without hearing some reference to either the need for prayer or the power
it wields. So why devote a whole chapter to it here? Don't most Church
members already understand that if they need help, they can pray?

Well, yes and no. My observation is that the true *purpose* of prayer is
often misunderstood or is at least incomplete. And if the way we engage in
prayer is rooted in a less-than-accurate or less-than-complete understanding,
the outcomes we experience in the wake of our petitions will likely fall short
of our expectations. Such misunderstanding may likewise result in our failing
to recognize the answers the Lord is trying to provide. Our *approach* to prayer
can dilute our ability to receive and recognize the very power we seek by
praying. As a result, in the moment we most need increased comfort, strength,
peace, insight, or resolution from our Heavenly Father, our misperception

keeps us from having that experience. If this happens to us consistently, we might conclude our prayers are not being heard or answered. That leaves us vulnerable to having our faith in the Savior weakened at a time we need it strengthened.

This principle came into clearer view for me many years ago when I experienced a difficult work relationship that affected my self-esteem. In the early part of my career, I worked for someone who was very successful in business but a failure in the way he treated other people. He used his authority and position to routinely diminish and control those who worked for him, including me. I was increasingly negatively affected by his approach. My interactions with him left me feeling discouraged, inadequate, and full of self-doubt. I was frequently on edge and preoccupied by the relationship. But it was complicated. I worked with some good people, including a close friend, and the long-term prospects of the opportunity were promising. Consequently, it was not as simple as just walking away.

Often, I would share with my wife my feelings of frustration about this relationship. After several months of experiencing this internal struggle, one day I said to her, "What bothers me most is that I let him affect me this way. I shouldn't allow someone else to determine how I feel about myself."

Now, before I tell you how I dealt with this situation, I want you first to envision yourself in this circumstance. How would you approach your Heavenly Father for help? What would be the focus of your prayers? Would you ask for your boss's heart to be softened, that he would treat you differently? Would you pray that he could find greater happiness in his life so he would start dealing with people more fairly? Or would you maybe ask that something bad might happen to him so he would learn his lesson, kind of like the experience Scrooge had in Dickens's famous *A Christmas Carol*?

Certainly, all those things crossed my mind. My first impulse was to pray that something outside myself—the circumstance, the other person— would be changed. I suspect that is how most people would respond. When we face difficulty, our instinct is to ask our Heavenly Father to remove the thing that is causing us pain. If we are sick, we ask that we might be made well. If we are out of work, we ask that the next interview might lead to a job. All of this is natural, and I am not suggesting it is wrong to ask for such blessings when we pray.

Let's consider, however, how we might change the premise of our prayers to deal with the kind of circumstance I just described. Let's start by identifying the *real* problem I was experiencing. In other words, in my situation, what was the core issue I needed to confront, and what did I need to *experience* for it to be resolved? By asking myself that question, I came to realize that whether or not it was natural or even appropriate to want my boss to change, that was not what *I* really needed. Why? Because there would always be people in my life who could affect how I felt about myself if I allowed them to. The issue was not my boss. The issue was how I *permitted* him to make me feel.

At that time, what I *needed* was an enabling influence beyond my own that could reconcile my feelings of inadequacy and lift the burden I was carrying. I needed my emotions healed and to regain perspective about my eternal identity. Those were outcomes I could not engineer alone. I came to realize the remedy lay in a power I understood intellectually but with which I now needed a more personal experience. It was something only the Savior's Atonement could resolve.

Those thoughts led me to this question: "What does *the Lord* want for me in this situation (as opposed to "What do *I* want for me")?" As I considered that question, here is what I concluded:

1. He wants me to rise above this situation and to learn from it.
2. He wants me to be at peace, even amid my difficulty.
3. He wants my relationship with *Him*, not the actions or attitudes of my boss, to guide how I feel about myself.

Notice that none of those conclusions had anything to do with punishing or changing the behavior of the person I identified as the cause of my grief. That insight changed my perspective. It helped me recognize that *my boss's* behavior was not the core issue I needed to resolve or upon which I should focus my energy. The problem was *in*side, not *out*side, of me.

This acceptance led me to adopt a different approach in my prayers. I simply told the Lord I was unable to overcome my feelings of inadequacy on my own. I asked that those feelings be replaced with a spirit of calm and inner security. I pleaded for a sense of peace and asked that my spiritual confidence be restored. I also prayed about my attitude toward my boss and asked for help in overcoming the ill will I felt. Throughout, I specifically asked that the power of Christ's Atonement help me close the gap between self-doubt and self-confidence I had been unable to bridge on my own.

After a few weeks of applying this new perspective in my prayers, one day it dawned on me that I no longer felt the same level of concern and inadequacy that had been plaguing me. Although I still experienced periodic dissonance, it was not chronic as it had been before. I seemed to have had my own Enos moment when my pain was "swept away" (Enos 1:6). Like Enos, I came to know for myself that Christ's Atonement is real, because I had just *experienced* it. I recognized that *I* was not the one who had removed the pain but that *Christ* was. There was no other explanation for the change that had taken place. I also realized that the turning point in my experience had come when I changed the focus of my prayers.

In the weeks and months that followed, I adopted new tactics to deal with my boss—ones rooted in the new confidence I felt. I pushed back on certain demands while simultaneously making sure I brought significant value to the role I was performing for the organization. In time, his respect for my abilities prompted him to rely on my talents to advance important initiatives for our business. He came to see and use me as a valued resource.

But here's the most critical point. My boss did not alter his behavior. The lesson I learned was that his attitude and actions no longer really mattered. Through the strength of the Lord I garnered by changing my approach to prayer, I was able to alter the way *I* responded to my boss's behavior and how I was affected by it. And that response increased his respect for me. More importantly, it increased the respect I had for myself.

Taking a Fresh Approach

Perhaps we can use the principles I learned during this experience to deepen our understanding of prayer. Specifically, let's consider how prayer can help us more fully access the gift of grace as we encounter the temptations, challenges, and afflictions inherent in mortality. To make sure we undertake this examination properly, we should start with a clear and accurate definition of prayer, one that can help us better understand its purpose and the premise upon which we should base our approach to it. I believe one of the clearest definitions is found in the Bible Dictionary:

> As soon as we learn the true relationship in which we stand toward God (namely, God is our Father, and we are His children), then at once prayer becomes natural and instinctive on our part (Matt. 7:7–11). Many of the so-called difficulties

about prayer arise from forgetting this relationship. *Prayer is the act by which the will of the Father and the will of the child are brought into correspondence with each other. The object of prayer is not to change the will of God but to secure for ourselves and for others blessings that God is already willing to grant but that are made conditional on our asking for them.* Blessings require some work or effort on our part before we can obtain them. *Prayer is a form of work and is an appointed means for obtaining the highest of all blessings.* (Bible Dictionary, "Prayer," emphases added.)

Most of us understand and believe that when we pray, we are speaking to a Father who loves and wants to bless us. However, frequently, that is as far as we take it. As a result, when we pray, we often convey an expectation that our dilemma or trial be reconciled by either altering our circumstances or simply removing the barrier completely. This is not unlike the child who comes home from elementary school and asks (expects) his parents to switch him to a different class because he doesn't like his teacher. When the parent does not acquiesce, the child assumes his mom or dad must not love or care about him enough or that they just don't get it. Similarly, when we pray and the outcome does not match our expectation, we might conclude that our prayer was not answered or, worse, that our Heavenly Father is not actually concerned about our well-being and success.

By drawing that conclusion, we exhibit our ignorance of the second part of the equation, which is that prayer is intended to align our will with the Father's. Note that this principle—unifying the will of the child and the Father—is the very essence of the Atonement (see Bible Dictionary, "Atonement"). Consequently, when we pray, our mindset and aim should be to bring "at-one-ment" our own desires with the purposes God intends for us (see Moses 1:39).

Let's go back now and apply this principle to the relationship I had with my boss. My relief came once I sincerely sought to know what the Lord wanted for me and once I became humble enough to seek His counsel, comfort, and strength. Once I surrendered to that way of thinking, the power of the Savior's Atonement and advocacy led me to a different way of viewing my needs and allowed Heavenly Father to forgive me for the lesser motivations I initially exhibited. Is it also possible that He allowed me to experience this adverse circumstance so I would learn how to more fully humble myself and more earnestly seek His help (see Ether 12:27)? Perhaps so.

What I learned through my experience is that we should allow our prayers to be guided by eternal *introspection*, not just eternal *perspective*. *Eternal*, in this context, means we look at ourselves and our circumstances as God does. He views us through the prism of our divine origin and eternal destiny (see chapter 2). So being guided by eternal introspection means we ask the right questions of *ourselves* before we approach our Heavenly Father in prayer. This kind of thinking will often lead us to pray for the capacity to endure pain and be at peace instead of just pleading for the obstacle or problem we face to be removed.

Principles of Acceptance and Surrender

The mindset we carry into our prayers determines whether we will truly seek the Lord's will in our petitions or be motivated by our own. It also influences our ability to recognize the answers He gives us line upon line and how prepared we will be to follow that counsel as it comes (see Matthew 4:18–20; 19:16–22; 2 Nephi 28:30). Nephi and Alma lived this principle and consistently sought greater alignment with God. Each provides insight born of their experience that can help us approach the Lord with a more open heart and willing mind. I call these insights the principles of *acceptance* and *surrender*.

Nephi introduces us to the principle of acceptance early in his writings. He tells us of his desire to see and understand the things his father had been shown in his vision of the tree of life (see 1 Nephi 10:17). His desire led him to pray and ponder. You will recall as he was thus engaged, he was carried away in the Spirit to a high mountain, where he was both interviewed and instructed by the Spirit of the Lord (see 1 Nephi 11:1). At one point during their interaction, Nephi and the heaven-sent messenger had this simple but highly significant exchange:

> And he said unto me: Knowest thou the condescension of God?
>
> And I said unto him: *I know that he loveth his children; nevertheless, I do not know the meaning of all things.* (1 Nephi 11:16–17, emphasis added)

Here Nephi introduces a perspective that should guide us in our approach to prayer. Nephi's trust in God was defined by two core beliefs: that God loves His children (and therefore He loved Nephi) and that Nephi did "not know the meaning of all things." The second insight is tempered by the first, is it not? If we know our Father loves us, it's okay that we "do not know the meaning of all things." We accept that the purpose of some things we experience in mortality will be unclear to us. But that's all right because we know our Father is mindful of us and is motivated by love.

It is important to note that Nephi was granted a deeper understanding of the condescension of God *after* his statement of acceptance. Because of Nephi's expression of faith, the Spirit could expand his perspective and reveal more truth (see 1 Nephi 11; Ether 12:6). Nephi not only saw what his father saw but was shown much more.

The second principle that should inform the perspective we bring to our prayers was introduced by Alma the Younger in his inspiring soliloquy:

> O that I were an angel, and could have the wish of mine heart, that I might go forth and speak with the trump of God, with a voice to shake the earth, and cry repentance unto every people. . . .
>
> But behold, I am a man, and do sin in my wish; *for I ought to be content with the things which the Lord hath allotted unto me*." (Alma 29:1–3, emphasis added)

Certainly, there was nothing unrighteous in Alma's desire. He wished to be unleashed from the constraints of mortality so he could more effectively share the gospel and bring souls to Christ. Yet, despite that worthy longing, he was constrained. Recognizing his mortal limitations and acknowledging what his Father *had* granted him, he was led to conclude that he should be content with that which he had been allotted.

This is a critical principle for anyone who wants prayer to magnify his or her experience with the Savior's Atonement. We, too, must come to view our present circumstance as what the Lord has allotted—and even rejoice in it. If it is what the Lord has granted, then it represents what we *need* right now. As a result, the question we should be asking is "What does the Lord expect me to be and do given what I have been allotted?" as opposed to "Why will the Lord not grant me more?"

Taken together, these two principles, acceptance and surrender, can help shape our perspective about our present circumstances and give us the strength to yield to what the Lord is trying to teach us. They suggest that in our present condition, we cannot completely understand the meaning of all things; nevertheless, we can be assured our Father loves us and that we have been allotted what He knows we need to experience for His purposes to be fulfilled concerning us.

These two principles draw their power from the demonstrations of faith they represent. Both Nephi and Alma expressed their trust in the Savior and exhibited a willingness to accept their present condition as an essential part of their spiritual development. It was that very frame of mind that gave them the power to press forward in carrying out God's plan concerning them. Because of their faith, *in time* their quests for greater insight and capacity were acknowledged and granted. However, it is not likely they would have fully recognized the blessings that ultimately flowed to them had they not first applied the principles of acceptance and surrender.

Where Do We Begin?

If we want our prayers to help us gain access to an expanded experience with atoning grace, where do we begin? How do we start regularly and effectively engaging in this practice, particularly if our prayers have become intermittent or shallow?

As with all spiritual matters, the starting point is belief. In fact, Alma taught that even if we can "no more than desire to believe," we should "let [that] desire work within [us]" to the point that we are willing "to experiment upon [the] word" (Alma 32:27; see also chapter 5) by starting to pray more meaningfully and regularly. As we do, prayer becomes a natural extension of our desire to have the Lord guide and direct us. Our persistence with the experiment of prayer will eventually bear fruit, and our testimony of this principle will expand. As it does, we will begin to experience the power of Christ's Atonement in ways we never thought possible.

CHAPTER 12

Take Time to Be Holy

If we yearn to dwell in Christ and have Him dwell in us, then holiness is what we seek, in both body and spirit. We seek it in the temple, whereon is inscribed "Holiness to the Lord." We seek it in our marriages, families, and homes. We seek it each week as we delight in the Lord's holy day. We seek it even in the details of daily living: our speech, our dress, our thoughts . . . We seek holiness as we take up our cross daily. (D. Todd Christofferson, "The Living Bread Which Came Down From Heaven," Ensign, November 2017.)

KEY UNDERSTANDING 12
When we consistently pursue greater holiness in our lives, light overwhelms the influences of darkness that can cause us to become mired in sin, worry, bitterness, or despair.

Daily Life

I received my call to serve as a bishop exactly one week before I was sustained in the ward. After I had accepted the call, my stake president asked me to prayerfully recommend two counselors to serve with me. Over the next couple of days, I spent much time thinking and praying about brethren who might be suitable to be called. After I had reached a preliminary decision, I decided I should go to the temple and seek the Lord's confirmation of what I had concluded.

It is impossible to describe the burden I felt at that time. I was overwhelmed by the prospects of my new role. And I did not yet have counselors with whom I could share the weight I was experiencing. I felt very alone. As a result, I wanted to be as close to the Lord as possible and looked forward to being in His house to receive guidance. I also thought the hour-long drive down the coastline would offer a good opportunity to think and pray. So, on the Tuesday night after the call had been extended to me, I made the trek to the San Diego temple to attend an evening session and pray about the brethren I thought should serve as my counselors.

In an effort to invite the Spirit as I made my journey, I listened to a CD of the Tabernacle Choir at Temple Square. One of the tracks on that recording was a hymn I had heard before but until that moment had not had any special significance for me. The name of the song was "Take Time to Be Holy." Because of the issues that weighed on me that evening, its lyrics resonated with me.

> Take time to be Holy, speak oft with thy Lord.
> Abide with Him always and feed on His word.
> Make friends of God's children, help those who are weak,
> Forgetting in nothing His blessing to seek.
>
> Take time to be holy, the world rushes on.
> Spend much time in secret with Jesus alone;
> By looking to Jesus like Him thou shalt be;
> Thy friends in thy conduct His likeness shall see.
>
> Take time to be holy, let Him be thy guide
> And run not before Him whatever betide.
> In joy or in sorrow still follow [the] Lord,
> And looking to Jesus trust in,
> Trust in the Lord.
>
> Take time to be holy, be calm in thy soul.
> Each thought and each motive beneath His control;
> Thus led by His Spirit to fountains of love,
> Thou soon shall be fitted for service above.
> Thou soon shall be fitted for service above.
> ("Take Time to Be Holy," *Submitted Music*, text by William
> D. Longstaff, arranged by Annette W. Dickman, 2007)

I replayed the hymn several times. With each subsequent listen, the Spirit I felt increased. I determined the song's message was a kind of clarion call and should become a guiding theme for my ministry as a bishop, both in what I taught and how I conducted myself. While I was experiencing this spiritual outpouring, I thought about the names of the brethren I had been considering as counselors. I received a sweet assurance that they were the right people to be called.

My subsequent temple visit that evening extended and magnified what I had experienced during my drive. It was one of the most meaningful visits to the Lord's house I have ever had. While there, I felt further confirmation that the counselors I had chosen were the ones the Lord had in mind. That validation came at a time I needed reassurance and a sense of peace about the responsibilities I was about to assume.

My journey to the temple that night gave me perspective about the role holiness needed to play in my life, regardless of my calling in the Church. It also left me feeling unified with the Savior. Consequently, as I embarked on my service as a bishop, I felt more "at one" with Him. In that sense, the very purpose of Christ's Atonement had been fulfilled in my behalf (see Bible Dictionary, "Atonement"; John 17:21–23).

Principles

It is important to understand that this story really has little to do with my call as a bishop. We do not have to be facing an assignment to nominate counselors to feel a need for the guidance and strength that can only come from being in a holy place and state of mind. Instead, my experience should be viewed as a metaphor for how we should respond to the experiences of mortality that test and humble us. During such times, we want heaven to be close. Because we cannot predict when moments of testing will come, we must continually and consistently refine our spiritual senses by intentionally cultivating holy practices in our lives.

That said, often a hardship we face can be the very thing that prompts us to engage in or return to holy practices. When we experience difficulty, it makes sense to pursue activities that will enable holiness to have a greater impact on our choices and thinking. Vulnerability can deepen our humility. And, when we are in a humbled state, the Lord can shape, guide, and ultimately heal us (see Ether 12:27; Helaman 3:35). He can *make* us holy.

A Tapestry of Holiness

The preferred solution to mortality's abundant challenges is to attain both a *sustained* and a *sustaining* experience with atoning grace, not just a periodic encounter. Yes, we want and need grace to hold us up and give us the strength to withstand the trials we face. But we also want and need that enabling power to last—to endure.

Gaining this kind of abiding, enabling power cannot be realized by occasionally participating in spiritual events or by simply focusing extra time and attention on one or two gospel principles, as valuable as those efforts might be (see 2 Nephi 31:19–20; Mosiah 4:1–7). Rather, an enduring experience with grace requires a willingness and ability to consistently reject impure influences and practices in favor of thoughts, activities, relationships, and behaviors that are holy. This is why *all* the principles discussed in this book are so important. Each adds an essential thread to the tapestry of a holy life.

Because the Lord wants the spiritual tapestry of our mortal experience to be vibrant and complete, He asks us to devote ourselves to holy practices. For this reason, He has given us the Sabbath to observe, the sacrament to partake of, and the temple in which to worship. He asks us to engage in these three activities so we can enjoy an *abiding* state of holiness and therefore a *sustained* experience with His grace. He knows that as we consistently participate in these sacred activities, we will gain enduring spiritual confidence and peace. Working together, these practices ensure that the other spiritual habits we form have a consecrating and purifying effect on us. The purpose of the Sabbath, the sacrament, and the temple is to help us experience the Savior's grace in a more intimate and lasting way.

So let's examine why this matters and how it is accomplished.

"Ye Shall Be Holy"

Anciently, the Savior gave this charge to the children of Israel: "For I am the Lord your God: ye shall therefore sanctify yourselves, and ye shall be holy; for I am holy" (Leviticus 11:44).

What does the Lord mean when He says, "Ye shall be holy; for I am holy"? His statement can be interpreted two ways: One is that He is giving us a directive to measure up, to align our behavior with the standard of holiness. The other is that he is describing something we can become. *We* can become holy because *He* has the power to make us holy. So which is it?

The reality is we do not have to choose between these two interpretations, nor are they mutually exclusive. In fact, as we explore this principle, we will see that both apply. But for now, either reading suggests that God expects us to let go of all forms of ungodliness—impurity, cynicism, crudeness, bitterness, selfishness, anger, sin, distrust, guile, and any other manifestation of unrighteousness.

We become more holy by fine-tuning our spiritual senses and aligning our behavior with our divine nature and destiny. That is why the Lord wants us regularly involved in activities and patterns that can transform our thinking and purify our hearts and minds. He knows that the more we are exposed to holy places and practices, the clearer the behavioral standards that lead to a holy character will become to us. And those who live holy lives are blessed with an inspired perspective about their condition, regardless of what that condition might be.

BE YE SEPARATE

While in the world, we are continuously exposed to two opposing influences. One, of course, is Jesus Christ, who created the Earth and governs all that takes place here. The other is Satan and his followers, who were cast out of heaven for rebellion and seek to make all of humankind miserable "like unto [themselves]" (2 Nephi 2:27; see also Revelation 12:7–9; Moses 1:3–39). Each of these forces attempts to persuade us, turning our mortal experience into a kind of spiritual tug-of-war. The scriptures refer to this ongoing tension as an "opposition in all things" (2 Nephi 2:11), and it is what makes our agency possible.

The Savior knows holiness can take root in our lives only if we are able to sufficiently distance ourselves from the influence Satan tries to wield over us. In fact, this principle is so critical that historically God took the step of *physically* separating His chosen people from adversarial groups and practices that threatened their spiritual or temporal survival. He did this with Noah's family, the children of Israel, the Nephites, the Jaredites, and the pioneers in our dispensation. Each group embarked on a journey of separation that was designed to preserve and protect them.

In our day, the Lord has commanded us to take equivalent journeys of separation from influences that can restrict and damage us spiritually. But the journeys we are asked to take are not physical or geographic. They are internal. We take them by engaging in holy practices and standing in holy places, not by moving to a different location. The Savior described it this way:

> And now I say unto you, all you that are desirous to follow the voice of the good shepherd, come ye out from the wicked, *and be ye separate, and touch not their unclean things.* (Alma 5:57; emphasis added)

In this instruction, the Lord makes it clear that our separation journeys have little to do with where we live. Instead, He asks us to become purer in heart and steadfast in our obedience, despite the wickedness that surrounds us. As a result, our journeys of separation are different from those undertaken by our ancient brothers and sisters. Nonetheless, they must be just as intentionally pursued.

The Sabbath, the sacrament, and the temple are three of the separation journeys the Lord has prescribed for our day. They offer us the opportunity to enter a more holy state of being and partition ourselves from the forces of darkness. They are spiritual excursions that lead us back into the presence of the Lord, there to receive instruction, make and renew covenants, and become endowed with a protective shield of holiness that will keep us "unspotted from the world" (D&C 59:9). We return from these journeys empowered with refined spiritual senses and capabilities that enable us to resist the adversary. And as with the ancients, the Savior's intent in having us take these journeys is to bring us to a greater state of purity so He can pour out an extra measure of His grace. Through that endowment, we gain heaven-sent strength to endure and overcome all things.

The Sabbath: A Journey of Sanctification

To become holy and receive the blessings a state of holiness bestows, we must be purged of impurity. The process for achieving this condition is called sanctification. Here is how the Lord describes the need for this kind of cleansing:

> And thus ye shall become instructed in the law of my church, *and be sanctified by that which ye have received,* and ye shall bind yourselves *to act in all holiness* before me—
>
> Purge ye out the iniquity which is among you; *sanctify yourselves before me.*

> And ye are to be taught from on high. *Sanctify yourselves*
> and *ye shall be endowed with power*, that ye may give even as
> I have spoken. (D&C 43:9, 11, 16; emphases added)

John explained how the blood of Jesus Christ can cleanse and sanctify us: "But if we walk in the light, as he is in the light, we have fellowship one with another, *and the blood of Jesus Christ his Son cleanseth us from all sin*" (1 John 1:7; emphasis added).

What I think John is saying is that as we consistently keep the commandments (walk in the light), we initiate the cleansing process that purges us of impurity. That is what it means to be sanctified. And the power of sanctification is made possible by the Atonement of Jesus Christ because it is "the blood of Jesus Christ his Son [that] cleanseth us from all sin."

Sabbath day observance brings a restoring and requalifying power to our lives that enables the Holy Ghost to cleanse and purify us. But here is the miracle: That sanctifying effect does not come to an end on Sunday night. Our Sabbath journey has an abiding, refining, and empowering impact on our spiritual desires and instincts every other day of the week as well. It helps us remain clean and pure before God *always*. The commitment to holiness that our Sabbath observance represents makes us eligible for atoning grace, which can then make "weak things become strong unto [us]" (Ether 12:27).

THE SACRAMENT: A JOURNEY OF REMEMBRANCE AND COMMITMENT

Because we partake of the sacrament every Sunday, it is easy to become numb to its significance and sacredness. But to invite greater light into our lives, we must learn how to engage more deeply in this ordinance. We can begin by adjusting our thinking about what should take place in our minds and hearts as the bread and water are blessed and then passed to the congregation.

This principle became particularly clear to me when I served as a bishop and sat on the stand each Sunday, facing the congregation as the sacrament was blessed and passed. That experience gave me a unique perspective about the significance of this ordinance to ward members. From that vantage point, I observed a rather wide disparity among the congregation about how we should conduct ourselves during this ordinance and the impact it should have on our lives. What I observed one Sunday in particular offers a good example of the range of understanding members had about the significance of the sacrament.

To set the stage, let me first offer some context. The teacher's quorum of our ward was asked to stand at the doors that led into the chapel and cultural hall during the administration of the sacrament each Sunday. Ours was a fairly large ward, so we typically had chairs set up into the cultural hall to accommodate everyone. For the most part, those young men did an excellent job with this assignment. However, periodically, there would not be enough teachers to man the posts, or someone would forget to stand at the door while the sacrament was blessed and passed.

When this happened one Sunday, while the bread was being passed to the congregation, a family came walking into the cultural hall through one of the side doors. The family made its way past the front row of chairs and headed up the center aisle to find seats. One of the young men that was passing the sacrament literally had to step aside so the family could get by. The father was still wearing his sunglasses, and the mother greeted several friends in the congregation as the group made its way to find seats, kids in tow.

I recall almost letting out an audible gasp. Virtually every eye in the back of the room was focused on this family as they made their way into the hall. I have no idea how many considered the timing of this family's entrance unusual or inappropriate, but it was apparent that those affected were no longer paying attention to their spiritual preparation and renewal. Certainly, Christ had ceased being the center of attention in that part of the congregation.

In contrast, as I observed members in the chapel and in other parts of the cultural hall, I saw several heads bowed and many individuals in obvious reflection. Some were looking at their scriptures and others at the words of the sacrament hymn just sung. It was as though these individuals were in a different realm than the family that came in while the sacrament was being passed, not just a different part of the same room.

Likewise, the young men blessing and passing the sacrament were models of reverence, order, and respect. Deacons were all dressed in clean white shirts and wore ties and appropriate dress pants and shoes. The priests all looked like missionaries in their suits. These Aaronic Priesthood holders did everything they should to create the right experience for the members.

Please understand. I felt no animosity toward those who came into the meeting during the passing of the sacrament on this or any other occasion. They meant no harm, and I am sure they were unaware of the disruption their late entrance caused. The family I reference in this example was experiencing some significant struggles, and I was pleased they were there at all. That said, I ached that more members failed to realize the significant opportunity the sacrament offers for them to commune with the heavens and be healed. Similarly, it pained me to think of how, as a ward, we discredited Christ's gifts by not properly reverencing the ordinance whose very purpose is to grant us access to the Atonement's enabling power.

As a result of this and other incidents, I periodically encouraged ward members to be a little more mindful of the sacred significance of the sacrament. My intent and hope was to enable them to experience Christ's Atonement more completely. I wanted them to remember that while participation in the sacrament *should* be a consistent pattern we engage in each week, it should *not* be a mere routine.

In contrast to the incident I just described, think of how our lives could be transformed if we were to treat the sacrament as though it were an invitation from the Savior to be with Him in the Garden of Gethsemane on the night He suffered in our behalf. To envision what might result from this kind of mindset, consider what Elder Orson F. Whitney experienced in the mission field, as recounted by Elder Jeffrey R. Holland:

> As a young missionary, Elder Orson F. Whitney (1855–1931), who later served in the Quorum of the Twelve Apostles, had a dream so powerful that it changed his life forever. He later wrote:
>
> "One night I dreamed . . . that I was in the Garden of Gethsemane, a witness of the Savior's agony. . . . I stood behind a tree in the foreground. . . . Jesus, with Peter, James, and John, came through a little wicket gate at my right. Leaving the three Apostles there, after telling them to kneel and pray, He passed over to the other side, where He also knelt and prayed . . . : 'Oh my Father, if it be possible, let this cup pass from me; nevertheless not as I will but as Thou wilt.'
>
> As He prayed the tears streamed down His face, which was [turned] toward me. I was so moved at the sight that I wept also, out of pure sympathy with His great sorrow. My whole heart went out to Him. I loved Him with all my soul and longed to be with Him as I longed for nothing else.

Presently He arose and walked to where those Apostles were kneeling—fast asleep! He shook them gently, awoke them, and in a tone of tender reproach, untinctured by the least show of anger or scolding, asked them if they could not watch with Him one hour. . . .

Returning to His place, He prayed again and then went back and found them again sleeping. Again He awoke them, admonished them, and returned and prayed as before. Three times this happened, until I was perfectly familiar with His appearance—face, form, and movements. He was of noble stature and of majestic mien . . . the very God that He was and is, yet as meek and lowly as a little child.

All at once the circumstance seemed to change. . . . Instead of before, it was after the Crucifixion, and the Savior, with those three Apostles, now stood together in a group at my left. They were about to depart and ascend into heaven. I could endure it no longer. I ran from behind the tree, fell at His feet, clasped Him around the knees, and begged Him to take me with Him.

I shall never forget the kind and gentle manner in which He stooped and raised me up and embraced me. It was so vivid, so real that I felt the very warmth of His bosom against which I rested. Then He said: 'No, my son; these have finished their work, and they may go with me; but you must stay and finish yours.' Still I clung to Him. Gazing up into His face—for He was taller than I—I besought Him most earnestly: 'Well, promise me that I will come to You at the last.' He smiled sweetly and tenderly and replied: 'That will depend entirely upon yourself.' I awoke with a sob in my throat, and it was morning." (Jeffrey R. Holland, "The Atonement of Jesus Christ," *Ensign*, March 2008.)

I am not suggesting we will experience what Elder Whitney did each time we partake of the sacrament. The odds are, most of us will never have that privilege. Nonetheless, we *can* approach the sacrament with the level of reverence and sanctity his dream represents. We can deepen our commitment to remember the Savior always. As we keep that promise, we too will feel the warmth of His love and long to be close to Him, as Elder Whitney did. That yearning will keep us on the path that leads to the fullest measure of His grace as we seek to endure and overcome the challenges we face.

THE TEMPLE: A JOURNEY OF EMPOWERMENT

During the sacrament, we express our *willingness* to take the name of Christ upon us. The terminology is interesting considering that at our baptism, we covenant *to take His name upon us*—not just our *willingness* to do so. So why the difference? Or is it really a distinction without a difference?

The saving ordinances and covenants of the gospel are progressive in nature. They move us from grace to grace in a process that is intended to help us overcome our natural man tendencies and become sons and daughters of Christ, even "new creatures," as the scriptures call it (D&C 93:12–14). Upon awakening from the revelatory coma he experienced, Alma the Younger explained what the Lord taught him about this kind of transformation:

> And the Lord said unto me: Marvel not that all mankind, yea, men and women, all nations, kindreds, tongues and people, must be born again; yea, born of God, changed from their carnal and fallen state, to a state of righteousness, being redeemed of God, becoming his sons and daughters;
>
> And thus they become new creatures; and unless they do this, they can in nowise inherit the kingdom of God. (Mosiah 27:25–26)

The Sabbath and the sacrament are an extension and continuation of our baptismal covenants. Their purpose is to prepare us for the more complete spiritual transformation temple ordinances are intended to effect. It is in the temple that our experience with the Atonement culminates and we become endowed with the fullest measure of the Lord's grace we can receive in this life.

The endowment we receive in the Lord's house is also progressive in nature. This progression occurs in three ways:

1. Through the things we are taught and the manner in which we are instructed
2. Through the ordinances we receive and the covenants we make
3. Through the endowment that is bestowed upon us

Holiness to the Lord: The House of the Lord

To better understand how the temple prepares us to take the Savior's name upon us and become endowed with power to be holy, we should focus first on the words written on its walls: HOLINESS TO THE LORD: THE HOUSE OF THE LORD. These phrases offer two critical clues about the experience we will have once we pass through the temple doors: what we will learn about (holiness) and in whose presence and home we will be taught (the Lord's). We will examine the latter first.

The phrase "House of the Lord" implies that when we pass through the temple doors, we are quite literally entering our Father's home on Earth. Each member of the Godhead can and does take up residence there (see *Guide to the Scriptures*, "Temple, House of the Lord"). Because of that truth, it is the perfect environment in which our Father can homeschool us in His patterns and priorities—just as He did when we were in His presence prior to coming to Earth.

In this divine schoolhouse, we engage in a celestial course of study in which Heavenly Father prescribes the curriculum, the Savior pays our tuition, and the Holy Ghost is our instructor, tutor, and guide (see John 14:26). Because instruction from on high is personalized, we are taught only the things we are prepared to receive, based on our present state of spiritual development (see D&C 43:16). In other words, the Holy Ghost both reveals and conceals truth as we progress through different phases of our spiritual education, and he tutors us in the way that will most benefit our growth, conditioned upon what we are able to understand *right now* based on our present state of development.

That said, at every stage of our temple instruction, the Savior's Atonement has an enabling and quickening effect. As a result, both those of advanced understanding and those just starting out on their temple journey receive a full endowment of the gifts the ordinances of the Lord's house bestow. In other words, one does not have to be a graduate student in one's temple experience and understanding to become a beneficiary of the promises, power, and blessings of their covenants. This is one of the magnifying gifts of grace. It is present at each stage of our temple experience and propels our understanding of celestial expectations and endowments.

The phrase "Holiness to the Lord" implies that our whole focus in the temple is intended to be on learning how we become holy *even as our Father is holy*. By its very nature, the Lord's house both represents and demands of us a certain way of being and living. In other words, the temple illustrates holiness in every aspect of its design and presentation while also requiring those who enter its doors to lay aside "every . . . unholy and impure practice" (Marion G. Romney, "The Voice of the Spirit," *Liahona*, April 1981). It models perfection and teaches us that we can one day be endowed with all the attributes our Father and His Son possess. Our temple journey illustrates how we can move from being perfect *in* Christ (fully reliant on the sufficiency of His mercy and grace) to becoming perfect *like* Christ (possessing the same holy character He has) (see Moroni 7:48; 10:32–33; D&C 93:1–3, 11–14; D&C 88:67–68).

Once we fully embrace this principle, so many things in our lives will naturally fall into place. If holiness is the standard and perfection the aim, the need for the patterns spoken of in chapter 4 becomes obvious. These patterns enable and sustain our holiness. We start to view the commandments as freeing instruments of transformation rather than barriers to our happiness. We long to know what the Lord would have us do each day to become more holy, because we know that is how we will become more like Him. As a result, we are more inclined to invite His guidance through purposeful prayer. We more naturally view our trials and temptations as sacred, refining experiences and seek to know what we are supposed to learn from them. Over time, our desires are refined and we long to be more like the Father and the Son in every way (see 3 Nephi 12:48).

But the role of the temple is not merely to show us the way to holiness. Its ordinances literally *endow* us with the power to *become* holy, fulfilling the very essence and purpose of the Savior's grace (see Bible Dictionary, "Grace"; D&C 38:32, 38; D&C 43:16.) In the temple we learn what a holy life consists of and how the Savior's expiation makes holiness possible, *and* we are empowered to *be* holy—to act "in all holiness" (D&C 43:9–10) each day of our lives. As we keep the covenants we make in the Lord's house, part of the power we receive is clarity about those things we need to do to be considered acceptable before the Lord—to be holy.

Here we return to the difference between a *willingness* to take the name of Christ upon us and actually *taking* it upon us. The ordinances and covenants of the temple teach us that Christ Himself *puts* His name upon us in His holy house. Through the washing, anointing, and endowment sequence, "the power of godliness is manifest" (D&C 84:20), and we are given the authority of Christ—even the power to act in His name and to represent His reality and example. This is not the same thing as worthy men being ordained to the priesthood and authorized to act in His name, although that is part of it. Rather, it is the authority to carry out the Savior's work in His name. And it is the endowment of power needed to rise above earthly evils and emulate the holiness of our Heavenly Father and His Son so we are able to do their work. President Dallin H. Oaks explained it this way:

> When the children of Israel were still on the other side of the Jordan, the Lord told them that when they entered the promised land there should be a place where the Lord their God would "cause his name to dwell" . . . Time after time in succeeding revelations, the Lord and his servants referred to the future temple as a house for "the name" of the Lord God of Israel. After the temple was dedicated, the Lord appeared to Solomon and told him that He had hallowed the temple "to put my name there for ever." (1 Kgs. 9:3; 2 Chr. 7:16.)
>
> Similarly, in modern revelations, the Lord refers to temples as houses built "unto my holy name" (D&C 124:39; D&C 105:33; D&C 109:2–5). In the inspired dedicatory prayer of the Kirtland Temple, the Prophet Joseph Smith asked the Lord for a blessing upon "thy people upon whom thy name shall be put in this house" (D&C 109:26). . . .
>
> The scriptures speak of the Lord's putting his name in a temple because he gives authority for his name to be used in the sacred ordinances of that house. That is the meaning of the Prophet's reference to the Lord's putting his name upon his people in that holy house. (See D&C 109:26.)
>
> Willingness to take upon us the name of Jesus Christ can therefore be understood as willingness to take upon us the authority of Jesus Christ. According to this meaning, by partaking of the sacrament, we witness our willingness to participate in the sacred ordinances of the temple and to receive the highest blessings available through the name and by the authority of the Savior when He chooses to confer them upon us. . . .
>
> Thus, those who exercise faith in the sacred name of Jesus Christ and repent of their sins and enter into his covenant and keep his commandments can lay claim on the atoning sacrifice of Jesus Christ. Those who do so will be called by his name at the last day. (Dallin H. Oaks, "Taking upon Us the Name of Jesus Christ," *Ensign*, May 1985.)

This truth helps us better understand the power that comes to us by living our lives according to the covenants we make in the temple. It also explains why we are invited to subordinate our will to God's during the endowment ordinance. The Lord knows that our power to become holy is directly linked to our ability to be submissive, humble, and meek and to be willing to do everything the Lord asks of us (see Mosiah 3:19; Helaman 3:35). This is because that is how the Savior grew from grace to grace (see D&C 93:1–6, 11–14). As we surrender our personal desires and ambitions and commit to aligning our thoughts and behavior with our Father in Heaven's will, we are brought more fully "at one" with Him (see John 17:11–13). In that state of humility and surrender, the Savior's atoning grace is able to *endow* us with the power to let go of our natural man tendencies in favor of a more celestial way of thinking and being.

In a very real way, then, the temple becomes the place where the very definition of the Atonement is fulfilled (see Bible Dictionary, "Atonement"). In the Lord's house, we are made complete (at one with God) through the mercy and grace the Savior endows upon those who participate in temple ordinances with a pure heart and unfeigned intent. As a result, our worship there brings about a more complete and enduring experience with the Savior's Atonement.

The Power of Being Set Apart

How is it possible that sincerely undertaking the three journeys—observing the Sabbath, partaking of the sacrament, and worshipping in the temple—spoken of in this chapter can grant us the power to remain unspotted from the world and overcome the temptations, trials, and tests of mortality?

The Sabbath, the sacrament, and the temple have been set apart, dedicated, and sanctified by the Lord. Those, then, who properly prepare to keep the Sabbath, partake of the sacrament, or enter the temple are entitled to the cleansing influence with which each of those experiences has been blessed by the Man of Holiness. Because those journeys have been sanctified by God, they possess the power to grant us a personalized, purifying experience as we keep the covenants associated with those holy practices.

And what is the source of purifying power? It is the Atonement of Jesus Christ. His sacrifice unleashed a power of cleansing—conditioned on our faith, repentance, and obedience. The Sabbath, the sacrament, and the temple point us to Christ and allow us to more fully take *His* yoke upon *us* (see Matthew 11:28–30). As we align our minds and hearts with His, we feel the power of His Atonement helping us do things we would not otherwise be able to do. That is why we should want to take these three journeys regularly and worthily.

WHAT ENOS LEARNED

And my soul hungered; and I kneeled down before my Maker, and I cried unto him in mighty prayer and supplication for mine own soul; and all the day long did I cry unto him; yea, and when the night came I did still raise my voice high that it reached the heavens. . . . And it came to pass that after I had prayed and labored with all diligence, the Lord said unto me: I will grant unto thee according to thy desires, because of thy faith. (Enos 1:4, 12)

BASED ON WHAT WE READ in his record, it is safe to assume Enos felt somewhat alienated from his Heavenly Father as he entered the woods to hunt. Presumably, he had unreconciled feelings and lacked insights he felt he needed but had not received. After all, he said his soul hungered, and he described his day-long pleadings as a wrestle before God. All of it paints a picture of someone engaged in serious introspection and finding himself coming up short.

That said, as we read Enos's entire record, it is evident that he was no weakling. He had enormous strength, and it is doubtful he lacked confidence. Yet he was meek enough to consider the things his father had taught and was sufficiently humble to recognize the need to improve his relationship with God. His heart was open to seeking greater light. His desires to resolve his spiritual dissonance prompted him to pursue greater holiness in the hope of attaining the blessings it offered. Certainly, we would all benefit from such a pursuit in our efforts to overcome the struggles or pain *we* experience.

But there is more to Enos's story and what we can learn from his experience. It is important to observe that Enos did not leave the things with which he struggled unresolved. He took steps to close the spiritual gap he was experiencing. He did not surrender to the darkness with which Satan certainly wanted to envelop him. Instead, he did all he could to invite greater light into his life. He drew upon the teachings he had been given. He hoped and exercised faith. He trusted there was something better ahead if he would persist in the right patterns—those that would invite enlightenment and dispel darkness and confusion.

Given the action he chose in the wake of his spiritual crisis, it is apparent Enos had been taught what he should do under such circumstances. He knew he needed to create an environment where the spirit could influence him, so he retreated to as sacred a place as was available to him—a place with which he was likely familiar and had probably visited during previous hunts. He likely knew what it would be like there and that he would have time to himself so he could be alone with his thoughts.

As he was hunting in the woods, he spent time pondering matters with which heaven concerns itself, specifically the things about which his father (a prophet) had spoken. He compared what he had learned with what he was feeling inside and found incongruity. So he prayed. He had probably prayed before but perhaps never quite like he did that day (and night) in the woods. On that day, he sought with all his being to obtain a more complete connection with his Heavenly Father and to reconcile anything that was amiss. "I will tell you of the wrestle which I had before God" (Enos 1:2), he says. As a result, he received this response: "thy faith hath made thee whole" (Enos 1:8). That answer confirmed for Enos the victory he had achieved over the darkness which had impeded him.

As we consider that outcome, we should also note what Enos did *not* do in response to his struggles. He did not just wait it out, hoping one day his feelings would somehow magically change. Instead, he acknowledged them and sought resolution. He did not become bitter and turn away from God; rather, Enos turned toward Him. He did not try to excuse his inadequacies. He accepted responsibility for overcoming them.

By taking the approach he chose, Enos had an experience that changed him. He was a different person when he left the woods than when he entered. He had put the principles and doctrines of the gospel to the test and found them to be both true and empowering. He confirmed that prayers are heard and answered. Light overcomes darkness. Holy places enable holy experiences. Christ's grace is real. God is merciful. Those truths changed everything for Enos, and they can do the same for you and me.

Assessment

To help you determine the extent to which you Fill Your Life with Light (Principle Four), consider completing this brief assessment. Give each statement a score between 1 and 10 (10 suggesting the statement describes you completely) based on your current state of mind and circumstances. Your scores will help you identify strengths you can build upon and barriers you need to address as you seek to overcome challenges and make spiritual progress.

1. I am conscious of and regularly assess the condition of my heart.
2. I recognize when I have a hardened heart and take steps to correct it.
3. I am not easily offended and routinely forgive others.
4. I embrace truth when I hear it instead of questioning or doubting it.
5. I am guided by the principles and characteristics of charity in my life (see Moroni 7:45).
6. I use prayer as a time of eternal introspection.
7. I pray to learn the Lord's will, not to seek my own.
8. I make a conscious effort to keep the Sabbath day holy.
9. I partake of the emblems of the sacrament with a broken heart and contrite spirit.
10. I worship God in the temple often and feel empowered by my temple covenants.

As you review your scores, which areas represent strengths you can build upon? Which are areas that could become potential barriers to your peace if not addressed?

Strengths to Build Upon:
1.
2.
3.

Potential Barriers to Peace:
1.
2.
3.

Consider making notes about the steps you plan to take to improve your application of this principle.

Actions:
1.
2.
3.

ALLOW CHRIST TO TRANSFORM YOU

MOST OF US HAVE A diluted understanding of the Savior's ability to make us equal to the tests of mortality. This incomplete understanding can result in an impaired perspective, weakened faith, and diminished hope. As indicated in this book's introduction, this misunderstanding is what causes many faithful members of the Church to suffer unnecessarily despite their belief in Christ.

The purpose of this final principle—allowing Christ to transform you—is to address the limitations we often place on the Savior's capacities to help and heal us. It is intended to increase our understanding of His grace, thereby giving us reason to have greater hope and faith (see 1 Peter 3:15). We will learn that He is not simply a helpful guide, teacher, and example. Because of the Atonement He performed, Christ can transform us from our weakened condition to a state of spiritual strength, enabling us to meet all the demands and trials we face. That was the purpose of His sacrifice, and it is how He uses the infinite power of His atoning grace for our gain (see 2 Nephi 2:1–2).

Because of agency, Christ will not force His influence upon us. Instead, we must invite Him to help us. We do that by demonstrating complete trust in Him and patiently pursuing a path that allows His grace to work its miracle in our lives, because that is what His Atonement empowered Him to do—perform miracles (see Moroni 7:27–33). He can mend and even change our hearts, help us overcome sin and weakness, fill us with comfort and peace, and ultimately make us perfect and complete.

When we live a faith-filled life, the Savior's grace is sufficient to save us from pain and grief and turn our sorrows into lessons in spiritual refinement that lead us to perfection (see Ether 12:27; Moroni 10:32–33). That is the plan. That is the purpose of His Atonement.

As a result, our experience with Christ's atoning grace will be complete when we have *become* that which the Savior's suffering empowers us to be. Moroni said it this way:

> Yea, come unto Christ, and *be perfected in him*, and deny yourselves of all ungodliness; and if ye shall deny yourselves of all ungodliness, and love God with all your might, mind and strength, *then is his grace sufficient for you, that by his grace ye may be perfect in Christ* . . .
>
> And again, if ye by the grace of God are perfect in Christ, and deny not his power, *then are ye sanctified in Christ by the grace of God*, through the shedding of the blood of Christ, which is in the covenant of the Father unto the remission of your sins, *that ye become holy, without spot. (Moroni 10:32–33, emphases added.)*

Given that the Savior has invited us to be transformed by Him, the only question remaining is whether we will accept that offer and grant Him permission to do so. Will we *allow* Him to work His miracle in us, or will we continue to depend upon our own strength and will to get through life? And assuming we want to do things the *Lord's* way, how do we invite that kind of transformation to occur, and how will we know whether it is, in fact, happening? To answer, let's turn our attention to the principles, patterns, and power associated with atoning grace.

CHAPTER 13
Receive the Gift of Grace

When we understand grace, we understand that God is long-suffering, that change is a process, and that repentance is a pattern in our lives. When we understand grace, we understand that the blessings of Christ's Atonement are continuous and His strength is perfect in our weakness (see 2 Corinthians 12:9). When we understand grace, we can, as it says in the Doctrine and Covenants, 'continue in patience until [we] are perfected' (D&C 67:13).

(Brad Wilcox, "His Grace is Sufficient," BYU Speeches, July 2011.)

KEY UNDERSTANDING 13

Grace is how Christ manifests the power of His Atonement in our lives. It is a gift that has no limits to its strengthening, comforting, enabling, healing, and redeeming power. Through His grace, Christ makes us spiritually whole.

Daily Life

One day in 2018, my wife and I received a call from our youngest child, who was twenty-one at the time. She was calling from work and was quite upset. That morning she had gone to retrieve her car in the parking garage of her apartment complex, and it was gone. It had been towed.

After securing a ride to work, she promptly called the impound company. She was told her car had been hauled away for being double-parked. As she protested, the towing company representative essentially rebuked her. He said that if she wanted her car back, she would need to come down to the yard and pay the fee. End of discussion.

Because our daughter was at work, she did not have time to follow up with the apartment leasing office or the impound company to make her case that, in her opinion, this was a gross injustice. She told her mother and me that she had left her car in a spot that many in her building had used before, and it was the vehicle she was blocking that had been parked illegally, not her. The other car was in an unmarked stall. She further indicated that the other car had been there for a couple of months and had not moved. As a result, to our daughter, the situation was completely unjust. In addition, the impound fee she faced was not something she could afford to pay. To make matters worse, if she did not retrieve her car soon, the fee would increase. She was totally distraught.

I told our daughter that I would call the towing company and see what I could figure out. My subsequent conversation with the representative there went like you would expect it to go under the circumstances. He was unsympathetic to the explanation I offered. Further, he would not accept payment over the phone and insisted someone would have to come to the impound yard, provide identification, and pay the fine in cash before the car would be released. With my daughter at work and without transportation, that was easier said than done. In short, the injustices seemed to be compounding.

After the call, I told my wife about the conversation. We talked about how stressed our daughter was—not just because her car had been towed but because of the financial implications involved. We agreed that the best solution was for us to just pay the fine and get the car back, thereby relieving the anxiety the situation had created for our child.

So my wife went to the impound yard, paid the fine, and returned the car to our stressed-out daughter.

The next day, I got another call from this same child. She wanted my advice on how to approach the apartment leasing office about getting reimbursed for the fine my wife and I had paid the day before.

"My advice is that you *not* pursue getting reimbursed," I responded.

"But it's not fair, Dad," my twenty-one-year-old insisted. "My car shouldn't have been towed. The other car was not in a regular parking stall, and I was—and that car wasn't going anywhere! It had been there for weeks!" I imagine anyone who has had a similar experience can relate to her feelings of violation and injustice.

I explained that one of the things to learn from this situation is that we will experience many injustices in our lives that are simply not worth trying to resolve, because the pursuit of justice will cause too much damage to our personal peace. And that price more than offsets any recompense we might receive by proving our case. I said, "Your mother and I have covered the cost so *you* don't have to. Just accept that gift, avoid parking in that same spot in the future, and move on."

I am doubtful the principle I was trying to teach sank in at that moment or that my daughter fully appreciated the gift she had just been given. But the principle was true, and the gift had been extended despite her inadequate understanding of what had just taken place.

Principles

My wife and I did not want our child spending needless energy trying to right the wrong she felt so strongly about. We knew any time she invested in that attempt would carry an emotional and spiritual cost that was unnecessary, because her mother and I had already taken care of the bill. Instead, we wanted her to accept the gift of peace of mind she had been offered.

Similarly, the Savior asks us to let go of our attempts to deal with life's challenges on our own and trust that He has already covered the cost and borne the pain caused by our grief and sorrows. He wants us to believe in and accept the miracle of His atoning grace. His desire is that we allow *Him* to fill our voids, heal our wounds, and remedy the injustices we cannot solve or overcome on our own (see Matthew 11:28–30).

Most of us do not have a problem understanding those truths *intellectually*. Instead, our struggle is that the doctrine of grace seems both incomprehensible and unimaginable. We cannot conceive that such a gift is possible, nor do we know how to open it, so to speak. We fail to recognize the power it already wields in daily existence or how to more fully lay claim on its promised blessings. As a result, we pursue righteous goals and attempt to overcome adverse circumstances by relying solely on our mortal capabilities, as if no Atonement had been performed and no divine assistance is available. We either power through our challenges by applying our limited intelligence and personal strength, or we give up and surrender to despair.

To further illustrate the lack of understanding and perspective most of us have regarding grace, let's consider an alternative response my wife and I could have given to our child's impound predicament. Imagine that instead of the solution we actually provided, we responded like this to our daughter when she called:

"You made this mess, so you'll need to just deal with the consequences. You are on your own, so figure out how to get yourself to the impound yard, pay the fine, and retrieve your car. Please don't call us or ask for our help, because this is a test, and we want to see what you're made of. If you call or start asking for things, your test score will drop, and you will risk failing the exam. We know you are still young and vulnerable, but we believe you can do this. Now, get moving—and good luck."

I am guessing you reacted unfavorably to that response and found it a bit harsh at best. And why is that? Presumably, it is because if you are a parent, you want your child to feel like they can call you if they have an issue. While you do not want them to act entitled, you do want them to understand they are not alone in trying to solve problems they encounter or dilemmas they face. You want them to benefit from your experience, wisdom, and resources to remove barriers that impede their progress.

Do we think our Heavenly Father feels differently? Often, we act as if we do. We approach life as though we expect our Heavenly Father and the Savior to respond to *us* about *our* challenges, weaknesses, and vulnerabilities like my wife and I did to our daughter in the fictional version of our conversation. When we adopt such a mindset, we are essentially saying we do not think Christ's Atonement applies to *us* or, at least, that He lacks the power to help us in any meaningful way. In either case, we assume there are limits to what the Lord can do for us in times of need. As a result, *we* restrict His ability to rescue us.

Consider the Savior's response to this perspective:

> For what doth it profit a man if a gift is bestowed upon
> him, and he receive not the gift? Behold, he rejoices not in
> that which is given unto him, neither rejoices in him who
> is the giver of the gift. (D&C 88:33)

The truth is the Savior's grace can provide relief in our times of adversity that is just as real as the relief our child received when she turned to her parents for help. Of course, the assistance Christ extends is more eternally significant, but its effect is just as enabling, and His willingness to provide it is just as reflexive. Unfortunately, like my daughter, we often fail to recognize or understand the implications of the gift we have been offered.

And it *is* a gift. When my wife and I paid the impound fees for our distraught child, we did not expect her to pay us back. We knew she could not afford to. Similarly, grace is free. It is not a loan. The Lord knows there is no way we can possibly repay the price He paid for us. The Savior suffered in our behalf because of His love for us (see 1 John 3:16; 4:19), a love so deep it is called infinite. His sole motivation is to make it possible for us to experience the joy that is the aim and purpose of our existence (see John 15:10–11; 2 Nephi 2:24–26).

That said, we should not conclude that because grace is free, the Savior does not have expectations of us. He most certainly does. However, what Jesus expects of us is both simple and achievable. He asks that we acknowledge and show appreciation for His gift. We do that by being obedient—by diligently striving to learn and follow His commandments. If we will accept that condition, He promises to grant us peace, comfort, strength, and joy (see Mosiah 2:22–24). He has also assured us we will not be handed a bill to pay when our mortal journey is over or any time before (see 2 Nephi 2:4; 2 Nephi 9:50).

So What Is Grace?

I think most of us feel ill-equipped to define grace. But if we do not come to some understanding of what it means, it will be difficult to benefit from its enabling nature. And if we fail to fully tap into its power, we will never have a complete experience with Christ's Atonement. Therefore, it is important that we seek to deepen our comprehension of what grace is as well as what it's *not*.

Despite what some of our Christian friends of other faiths espouse, grace does *not* mean freedom from spiritual expectations, nor does it grant us permission to do whatever we want by simply accepting Jesus Christ as our Savior. Rather, grace is a constant and comprehensive influence that grants us the capacity to meet the demands God has placed upon us during our time on Earth. It is what makes it possible for us to pass the test this probationary period represents. It is the means by which Jesus is able to transform mortality from an unjust *existence* into a merciful and even joyful *experience*. It is the channel that provides access to the healing, enabling, forgiving, and strengthening power Christ's Atonement made possible.

Grace grants us divine assistance to fulfill our mission on Earth and conquer the temptations and challenges we encounter. It intervenes to compensate for the gaps in our lives that cannot be filled by merely exerting our own will and intellect. And the only thing grace demands of us in return is that we turn to Christ in our thoughts and deeds with a broken heart and a contrite spirit (see 3 Nephi 9:20). That's it. From there, grace takes over, assuming we allow it to.

To make grace a little more understandable, let's compare it to the principle of freedom. When we live in a free society, we have the ability to pursue

38

any outcome we want as long as we do not infringe on others' liberties. And even if we do not live in a society that grants personal freedom, we still have control over what we think and believe.

Freedom is a power that exists whether we take advantage of it or not. And it has both external and internal implications. In other words, there are no *external* limitations placed on what we can achieve through freedom's power. The only limits are those we self-impose (*internal* limitations) by not taking advantage of the opportunities freedom offers.

We cannot derive power from freedom by simply declaring we are free. Likewise, we cannot derive power from Christ's Atonement by merely saying we are saved. For freedom to benefit us, we must think, plan, work, develop our skills and talents, struggle, endure, and proactively seek out resources that will help us rise to our full potential (e.g., education, training, a vocation, technology, research, books, periodicals, mentors, and so forth). In other words, we activate freedom's power by exercising our agency toward productive and meaningful ends. Until we do, freedom remains dormant and untapped.

Although freedom grants us the power to become whatever we want, it does not guarantee or bestow any particular outcome unless we choose to use it as an enabling force to progress and grow. At the same time, our hopes, dreams, and talents would have no means of fulfillment without freedom, because we would not have the power to pursue them. However, because freedom does, in fact, exist as a constant and pervasive influence, we can access it at any time to alter our course or pursue our ambitions.

So it is with grace. It has the power to dispense a healing and a strengthening capacity to us whether we choose to access it or not. It derives that power from the Savior's Atonement and stands as a perpetual gift to anyone willing to put it to good use. Like freedom, grace's only limitations are the ones we place on it. It is powerful and comprehensive enough to enable us to move and breathe and otherwise make our way through each phase of our lives. But it is also subtle enough to stay out of our way until invited in. It will not violate our agency.

Just as freedom keeps us from being enslaved by external forces and allows us to elect how we will use our time and means, so grace is always in the background sustaining our mortal and spiritual capacities—even granting us the power to breathe moment to moment (see Mosiah 2:21). It emanates from God Himself, who stands ready to infuse us with increased aptitudes, comfort, relief, and the strength to do things our mortal perspective and logic tell us we cannot do. But as with freedom, we can choose to tap into grace to accelerate our spiritual progress and healing, or we can let it remain dormant.

The Bible Dictionary explains grace this way:

> The main idea of the word is divine means of help or strength, given through the bounteous mercy and love of Jesus Christ.
>
> It is . . . through the grace of the Lord that individuals, through faith in the Atonement of Jesus Christ and repentance of their sins, receive strength and assistance to do good works that they otherwise would not be able to maintain if left to their own means. This grace is an enabling power that allows men and women to lay hold on eternal life and exaltation after they have expended their own best efforts.
>
> Divine grace is needed by every soul in consequence of the Fall of Adam and also because of man's weaknesses and shortcomings. However, *grace cannot suffice without total effort on the part of the recipient.* Hence the explanation, "It is by grace that we are saved, after all we can do" (2 Ne. 25:23). It is truly the grace of Jesus Christ that makes salvation possible. (Bible Dictionary, "Grace," emphasis added)

Grace, then, both requires our effort and provides the strength we need to make that effort. In that sense, it is perpetuated and magnified through a self-reinforcing cycle. The more we seek to do our part by following spiritual patterns and keeping the commandments, the greater the endowment of grace ("strength and assistance") we receive. And the more we experience grace, the easier it is to maintain an eternal perspective about our circumstances, which in turn motivates us to continue our righteous habits.

In His metaphor of the vine and the branches, the Savior offered this insight regarding the progressive nature of His grace:

> I am the vine, ye are the branches: *He that abideth in me, and I in him, the same bringeth forth much fruit: for without me ye can do nothing.*
>
> If ye abide in me, and my words abide in you, *ye shall ask what ye will, and it shall be done unto you.*

Herein is my Father glorified, that ye bear much fruit;
so shall ye be my disciples.

As the Father hath loved me, so have I loved you: *continue ye in my love.*

If ye keep my commandments, ye shall abide in my love;
even as I have kept my Father's commandments, and abide
in his love.

These things have I spoken unto you, that my joy might
remain in you, *and that your joy might be full.* (John 15:5,
7–11, emphases added)

I am struck by how much emphasis Christ places on three words in
these verses about grace: love, joy, and abide. Those terms evidence the
purity of the Savior's motive in offering His atoning power to us. He
recognized that mortality would be difficult and even impossible to endure
if there were not a safety net to catch us when we fall as we make our way
on Earth. His love for us is so great that He was willing to suffer for us so
our suffering would not only be limited but swallowed up in *joy.* As a result,
He invites us to abide in Him by keeping His commandments.

INVITING GRACE INTO OUR LIVES

So if grace is always present and we cannot actually earn it, what must we
do to invite its influence and access its power? Certainly, our efforts play some
role in grace's ability to help us as we navigate mortal tests and temptations.
But what does that effort include and what form should it take?

The answer to those questions starts with something very fundamental.
The first step in accessing the power of grace is to believe we are worthy of
the Savior's assistance. Here, I do not mean worthy in an eligibility sense,
as in being worthy to hold a temple recommend. Instead, I mean we accept
that the Savior's Atonement was performed for us *too*—that we are not an
exception or somehow beyond the reach of Christ's redeeming power and
love. There is nothing that can render us ineligible to be rescued by Him or
that can remove us from His love (see Jeffrey R. Holland, "The Laborers in
the Vineyard," *Ensign*, May 2012).

We are worthy of Christ's help simply because He *does* love us—even, and
perhaps especially, when we feel unworthy of His love. President Dieter F.
Uchtdorf explained it this way:

Our Savior, the Good Shepherd . . . knows and loves you.

He knows when you are lost, and He knows where you are. He knows your grief. Your silent pleadings. Your fears. Your tears.

It matters not how you became lost—whether because of your own poor choices or because of circumstances beyond your control.

What matters is that you are His child. And He loves you. He loves His children. (Dieter F. Uchtdorf, "He Will Place You on His Shoulders and Carry You Home," *Ensign*, May 2016.)

Once we accept that we are worthy of the Savior's grace, our next step is to turn to Him. This simply means that we exercise some degree of faith, even if it is no more than a desire to believe that Christ can help us (see chapter 5). That is what hope is. It is yearning deeply enough to take righteous action in *anticipation* of receiving promised blessings we have not yet fully experienced—at least not in a way we recognize (see Alma 32:27; Hebrews 11:1).

And so, when a loved one dies, we exercise hope that our grief will subside and then act as though it already has by focusing on and assisting others. We *hope* we can overcome our guilt and feel at peace, so we take action by repenting. We *hope* we can endure the physical, emotional, or spiritual pain we experience, so we act in faith by receiving a priesthood blessing and seeking the help and advice of priesthood leaders and medical professionals. When we take action that is rooted in hope, we demonstrate our *willingness* to humble ourselves and turn to God.

So how *do* we then turn to God as an expression of our hope?

We do so by increasing our righteousness. Whatever *next* step we need to take to align ourselves with the Lord's teachings and commandments, that is what we do. For some of us, that may mean scheduling time with our bishop to begin the repentance process. For others, it may mean starting to pray or praying with purer motives and real intent. We may need to begin attending our church meetings more regularly or serving in our church callings more diligently. Maybe we need to deepen our temple worship or increase the level of charity we show toward others. Many of us will need to forgive someone, be less judgmental, or otherwise purge ourselves of guile.

In short, while keeping the commandments is the universal formula for increasing our righteousness and accessing grace, the specific steps we each need to take in that regard will depend on our individual circumstance. Each of us needs to be willing to turn to the Lord and ask the same question the rich young man posed: "What lack I yet?" (Matthew 19:20; see also Matthew 19:21–22). And we must want the answer. Then we have to be willing to act on the direction the Lord gives us (see D&C 84:46). By following the patterns discussed in chapter 4, we demonstrate that willingness—that we are earnestly pursuing the path of righteousness. As a result, we will feel and recognize the power of grace in our lives.

CHAPTER 14
Claim the Fruits of Grace

Please learn that as you wrestle with a challenge and feel sadness because of it, you can simultaneously have peace and rejoicing. Yes, pain, disappointment, frustration, and anguish can be temporary scenes played out on the stage of life. Behind them there can be a background of peace and the positive assurance that a loving Father will keep His promises. You can qualify for those promises by a determination to accept His will, by understanding the plan of happiness, by receiving all of the ordinances, and by keeping the covenants made to assure their fulfillment.
(Richard G. Scott, "Trust in the Lord," Ensign, November 1995.)

KEY UNDERSTANDING 14
Grace does not necessarily remove the obstacles we face in mortality. When it doesn't, it provides us strength, reassurance, comfort, and confidence while we experience those trials.

Daily Life

A single sister I was meeting with regularly in my role as her bishop was undergoing significant ongoing challenges. Her struggles included chronic health issues, employment concerns, and financial pressures. In addition, one of her adult children was dealing with legal problems that demanded much of her time and financial support. To cap it off, her former spouse was emotionally unstable and could, without warning, wreak havoc in her life for a day, a week, or longer.

Most of my meetings with this single mother centered on finding solutions to the multiple struggles she was trying to navigate and helping her cope with them. Because of the scope and intensity of the issues she was dealing with, I had particular concern for her spiritual welfare. During one of our conversations, I asked how her testimony was holding up under the pressure she was experiencing. Her response was insightful: "Oh, Bishop, my testimony is strong. I know the Lord is mindful of me and my family," she said. "I have had so many experiences that have witnessed that to me."

She proceeded to talk about the profound spiritual resolution she felt when first introduced to the gospel many years prior—and the many instances since when she had seen the Lord's hand at work in her life. She said she continued to feel His tender mercies and was quick to acknowledge the Savior's sustaining influence. She had an inspired perspective about her circumstances. She was devoid of any guile or bitterness.

Her frame of mind confirmed two important truths: Inner peace does not mean an absence of adversity. And it is not the purpose of grace to clear our path of all obstacles, temptations, or trials. Rather, peace is one of the gifts grace bestows upon the righteous when they remain steadfast despite their challenges. It results from having our "confidence wax strong in the presence of God" because of our faith-fueled, hope-inspired approach to life (see D&C 121:45–46). Peace comes to us when we know where we stand with God, understand His ways and nature, and submit our will to His, just as Christ did in His darkest hour:

> And he went a little further, and fell on his face, and prayed, saying, O my Father, if it be possible, let this cup pass from me: *nevertheless not as I will, but as thou wilt.* (Matthew 26:39, emphasis added)

Principles

When we experience something that is hard to bear, it is not easy to maintain the perspective this good sister had. During such periods, our natural inclination is to either retreat from productive behavioral patterns and positive relationships or to become altogether paralyzed by our circumstances (see chapter 1). When this happens, it becomes harder to recognize the tutoring hand of the Lord at work. We can likewise become blind to the way His grace sustains us, the refining effect it has on our character, and the purifying influence it has on our souls. This can then lead us to believe that it is merely our intelligence and resolve that is getting us through a tough period, not understanding how much harder it would be were the Savior not lifting us up and lessening the impact of our burden.

In short, when we experience turmoil, it is easy to conclude that the Lord is not engaged in our lives. This usually happens because His help is not being provided in the way we expect or desire. As a result, we think *He* has distanced Himself from *us*, when in fact the opposite has occurred. By misreading the purpose of the adversity we experience, *we* have abandoned *Him*. We fail to understand that grace is always at work performing its *perfecting* role (see James 1:2–4). The problem is we simply don't recognize it.

The reason this happens is because most of us lack an understanding of how grace manifests itself. No one holds up a sign, and there is no audible voice saying, "Hey, you are experiencing grace now, so pay attention and appreciate what is going on!" Instead, grace has a modesty about it and requires refined spiritual senses to recognize it. And because many of us do not perceive its influence as it is going about its work, we stop reaching for the Savior's extended hand or seeking the help He stands ready to provide. Again, this is why many believe in the Savior and His Atonement yet remain in pain.

Given what is at stake, it would seem important that we correct the misconceptions we have about how the Savior's atoning gift influences us. Because if we can gain a clearer understanding of how grace is manifest, we can more fully experience its fruits, which, of course, means we will simultaneously have a more complete Atonement experience. So let's dive a little deeper and see if we can clear up some of the misunderstandings we have.

NOT AS THE WORLD GIVETH

When I was a bishop, many who came to discuss their challenges with me did not have the perspective of the single sister whose testimony did not waver during her trials. Instead, they were going through what I would call a crisis of faith, which was creating a kind of spiritual blindness. Mortality had become a lonesome and even *loath*some experience. They felt a spiritual and emotional void that was at odds with Christ's capacity and desire to succor and rescue them. That desire was never more eloquently stated than on the eve of His atoning sacrifice: "Peace I leave with you, my peace I give unto you: *not as the world giveth*, give I unto you. Let not your heart be troubled, neither let it be afraid" (John 14:27, emphasis added). On that same evening, He also promised, "I will not leave you comfortless: I will come to you" (John 14:18).

This reassurance was offered by One whose capacity to heal fear, bitterness, pain, sorrow, guilt, discouragement, and every other mortal infirmity was forged in His Gethsemane and Golgotha experiences, as well as through the afflictions He endured during His earthly ministry. As a result, it is a credible promise. The Savior's acts of sacrifice in our behalf imbued Him with love, mercy, compassion, and a desire to bless us with His grace (see D&C 122:8; Alma 7:12). Paul described Him as a high priest who is "touched with the feeling of our infirmities" and invited us to "come boldly unto the throne of grace, that we may obtain mercy, and find grace to help in time of need" (Hebrews 4:15–16).

However, in His promise to send us peace, there was a modifying phrase the Savior included. He said it would come "not as the world giveth." Those words imply the Savior's comfort will be offered in *His* way, on *His* terms, and according to *His* timetable but would, nonetheless, be extended for *our* good and benefit (see 2 Nephi 2:1–2; D&C 76:5, D&C 122:7). This is consistent with what He taught us through the prophet Isaiah:

> For my thoughts are not your thoughts, neither are your ways my ways, saith the Lord. For as the heavens are higher than the earth, so are my ways higher than your ways, and my thoughts than your thoughts. (Isaiah 55:8–9)

Surrendering to this truth brings its own comfort. We are invited to place our trust in someone who sees things we cannot see, always acts in our best interest, and has experienced everything we endure and more. What better tutor and guide could we possibly have?

During times of struggle and pain, it is easy to lose sight of this truth. When that happens, we can find ourselves counseling the Lord instead of seeking to be counseled (see Jacob 4:8–10). We do this, in part, by asking for solutions or expressing expectations that may be incompatible with the learning experience the Lord is providing. We end up circumventing the lesson He is trying to teach us.

The extension of this kind of thinking is the belief that for grace to be relevant, it must remove the obstacles that stand in the way of our peace. For example, if someone is harming us, we believe grace demands that person be immediately punished. If we have a disease or disability, we expect grace to heal us. If we have lost our job, grace should produce a new one—and quickly. In other words, we interpret grace to mean we can expect either a removal or absence of the conflict and adversity we face, or to the extent that it exists, it will be quickly resolved in a way that makes us more comfortable. After all, didn't Lehi say, "men are, that they might have *joy*" (see 2 Nephi 2:25, emphasis added)? What do suffering and extended trials have to do with joy?

I imagine some would *say* that the expectations just described are exaggerated—that most of us do not really think that way. They would argue we are much more measured in our reaction to adversity. However, if we are honest, how we actually *respond* when confronted with mortality's tests usually reflects at least a desire that grace work that way. In the face of difficulties, we want solutions to be immediate and comprehensive.

Because of this expectation, we often miss the opportunity to learn the true nature of God and how He goes about fulfilling His purposes in our behalf (see John 17:3). We fail to recognize that grace has a divine tutoring and purging role and is not simply a healing or repairing agent. It is a sustaining power that strengthens us *in* our struggles, not a magic elixir that removes them.

To put an exclamation point on this principle, let's return to the metaphor the Savior offered of our relationship to Him as branches attached to a vine. Leading up to the verses quoted in the previous chapter, we read this:

> I am the true vine, and my Father is the husbandman.
> Every branch in me that beareth not fruit he taketh away: and every branch that beareth fruit, *he purgeth it, that it may bring forth more fruit.* (John 15:1–2)

Isn't it interesting that the Lord says He *purges* the branch that "beareth fruit"? That seems counterintuitive, right? If we are producing fruit, we assume we should be rewarded with an outpouring of blessings—not laden with challenges and tests. But what reason does the Lord offer for purging us? "That [we] may bring forth more fruit."

The principle the Savior is teaching here is that He grants us the full fruit (blessings) of our faith and diligence "by and by" (see Alma 32:41–43). In the meantime, His grace endows us with an enduring power to bear the burdens we face. It is the compensating force He knew we would need during the tutoring and testing phases of our mortal experience—those that would cause us pain but would also imbue us with greater strength, wisdom, and charity. Through His grace, the Savior *ultimately* rewards our faith with the fruit of eternal life that Alma described as "most precious, which is sweet above all that is sweet, and which is white above all that is white, yea, and pure above all that is pure; and ye shall feast upon this fruit even until ye are filled, that ye hunger not, neither shall ye thirst" (Alma 32:42).

Returning to the Savior's metaphor, we find this direction:

> Abide in me, and I in you. As the branch cannot bear fruit of itself, except it abide in the vine; no more can ye, except ye abide in me.
>
> I am the vine, ye are the branches: He that abideth in me, and I in him, the same bringeth forth much fruit: for without me ye can do nothing. (John 15:4–5)

Grace is the nourishment we receive when we stay attached to the vine. As we respond to challenges with faith-filled obedience, we will feel replenished and encouraged. We will gain the strength to overcome what seems insurmountable and find ourselves able to move forward "notwithstanding [our] weakness" (2 Nephi 33:11). Ultimately, through our "abiding" efforts, we will "bring forth much fruit."

Tender Mercies

One of the ways the Lord grants us peace "not as the world giveth" is through something the scriptures call tender mercies (see 1 Nephi 1:20; Ether 6:12; James 5:11). Such endowments of grace are usually delivered in subtle ways that are apparent only to the spiritually aware. In the account I shared earlier in this chapter of the single mother, those mercies were manifested in the form of remembrances of spiritual encounters that sister had had when she was taught the gospel and throughout her life since. She was able to draw encouragement from those remembrances (see chapter 2). As a result, her reflex in times of difficulty was to continuously turn to the Lord for strength and support.

Elder David A. Bednar defined tender mercies this way:

> The Lord's tender mercies are the very personal and individualized blessings, strength, protection, assurances, guidance, loving-kindnesses, consolation, support, and spiritual gifts which we receive from and because of and through the Lord Jesus Christ. Truly, the Lord suits "his

mercies according to the conditions of the children of men" (D&C 46:15). (David A. Bednar, "The Tender Mercies of the Lord," *Ensign*, May 2005.)

If we want to increase our recognition of grace as it is manifest, we must take time to reflect on the tender mercies the Lord extends to us each day. As we do, we will see the many evidences He is providing of His specific, intimate, and ongoing involvement and the strengthening power we are receiving (see Alma 32:30). This insight likewise increases our understanding of grace. As that awareness is deepened, our faith is strengthened and our desire to be obedient is increased. Obedience expands our personal righteousness, which then compounds the outpouring of grace. This is how we grow from grace to grace until we no longer fear our circumstances or question the strengthening power the Savior continuously extends to us (see D&C 93:12–13).

Angels Still Minister

One of the most overlooked ways our Savior's grace is manifest is through the ministration and watchful care of His angels. The Lord has promised He will marshal those on the other side of the veil to assist, direct, comfort, and rescue us as we go about our mortal activities—especially when our tests are at their pinnacle. Consider these examples among many that could be given:

> I will go before your face. I will be on your right hand and on your left, and my Spirit shall be in your hearts, *and mine angels round about you, to bear you up.* (D&C 84:88, emphasis added)

> Behold I say unto you . . . *neither have angels ceased to minister unto the children of men.*
>
> For behold, they are subject unto him, to minister according to the word of his command, *showing themselves unto them of strong faith and a firm mind in every form of godliness.* (Moroni 7:29–30, emphasis added)

Of such heavenly ministrants, Elder Jeffrey R. Holland provided this reassurance:

In the course of life all of us spend time in "dark and dreary"
places, wildernesses, circumstances of sorrow or fear or discouragement . . . I testify that angels are *still* sent to help *us,* even
as they were sent to help Adam and Eve, to help the prophets,
and indeed to help the Savior of the world Himself. (Jeffrey R.
Holland, "The Ministry of Angels," *Ensign*, November 2008.)

If we wish to experience a greater measure of atoning grace during
difficult times, we must allow ourselves to believe that there are messengers
in our midst who are charged with extending the Savior's love and solace
to us (see 2 Nephi 32:2–3). This manifestation of the Lord's grace is most
visible to those who are following the righteous patterns we have discussed
in this book. The work of angels is real, but our awareness of their influence
is tied to the degree of spiritual sensitivity we have nurtured.

Finding Rest in the Lord

The Savior's mission and Atonement were performed so that we can
find sustained peace and rest—not just in the world to come but in this
life. In the Doctrine and Covenants, the Lord defines His rest as "the
fullness of his glory" (D&C 84:24). This is the ultimate state of grace our
Savior wants to bestow upon us. He wants to empower us to receive all that
our Father has and is—in full (see D&C 84:38). He said to Moses, "For
behold, this is my work *and my glory*—to bring to pass the immortality and
eternal life of man" (see Moses 1:39, emphasis added).

Although a *fullness* of God's glory can be obtained only in the next life,
most of us live far beneath our privileges to partake of its fruit in mortality as well. As indicated, the Lord's tender mercies offer us a glimpse of
His rest and glory. Perhaps more important, as we persist in patterns of
righteousness, the Lord fills us with confidence and assurance about our
state before him (see D&C 121:45–46), and through His grace, He grants
us the ability to be calm in our souls even as we experience adversity (see
D&C 123:17).

The Lord explained this principle to Joseph Smith in response to the
Prophet's plea for relief when he was confined in Liberty Jail:

My son, peace be unto thy soul; thine adversity and thine
afflictions shall be but a small moment;

And then, if thou endure it well, God shall exalt thee on high.

Let thy bowels also be full of charity towards all men, and to the household of faith, and let virtue garnish thy thoughts unceasingly; then shall thy confidence wax strong in the presence of God; and the doctrine of the priesthood shall distil upon thy soul as the dews from heaven.

The Holy Ghost shall be thy constant companion, and thy scepter an unchanging scepter of righteousness and truth; and thy dominion shall be an everlasting dominion, and without compulsory means it shall flow unto thee forever and ever. (D&C 121:7–8, 45–46)

This kind of spiritual confidence and assured state before God do not come to us all at once. Rather, they are built little by little as we patiently and deliberately nurture our spirituality day by day. Ultimately, a divine character is developed over a lifetime by consistently taking incremental steps toward a more righteous life, even during periods of intense challenge and temptation. As we remain "attached to the vine," over time we are sanctified in a way that is virtually imperceptible to us. That is why most of us do not recognize the full effect grace is having as it performs its perfecting work.

CHRIST WILL LIFT US UP

Perhaps the reason we have difficulty fully recognizing the presence of grace in our lives is because we cannot imagine a gift of such magnitude is possible, nor are we able to comprehend the depth of love that motivated the Savior to make the infinite sacrifice that gave birth to grace. The boundaries of our mortal reasoning limit us from grasping how it performs its work.

For these reasons and more, the premise of this book has been that the Atonement of Jesus Christ can be fully understood by *experiencing* it. That is why Enos was prompted to ask, "Lord, how is it done?" when his guilt had been "swept away" (Enos 1:6–7). He simply did not understand what had occurred. It was a new *experience* for him.

Because grace is such a hard principle for us to comprehend, our ability to *feel* its influence depends entirely on our willingness to believe and trust the Lord. The need for that trust reaches a zenith when our expectations are left unfulfilled—when life is just not turning out the way we planned, despite our best and most righteous efforts. Submitting to the Father's will in those circumstances is what unlocks the blessings of grace and leads us along the pathway of peace.

In the early stages of our spiritual development, it is important that we not become discouraged. The whole purpose of atoning grace is to lift us up and put us back on our feet every time we fall. The promise of the Savior is that He will strengthen us and grant us the ability to carry on (see Psalms 71:16; John 3:17; D&C 84:88). Elder Lynn G. Robbins said it this way:

> Knowing that the strait and narrow path would be strewn with trials and that failures would be a daily occurrence for us, the Savior paid an infinite price to give us as many chances as it would take to successfully pass our mortal probation. The opposition which He allows can often seem insurmountable and almost impossible to bear, yet He doesn't leave us without hope.
>
> To keep our hope resilient as we face life's trials, the Savior's grace is ever ready and ever present . . . His grace and His loving eye are upon us throughout our entire journey as He inspires, lightens burdens, strengthens, delivers, protects, heals, and otherwise "succor[s] his people," even as they stumble along the strait and narrow path. (Lynn G. Robbins, "Until Seventy Times Seven," *Ensign*, May 2018.)

The scope and purpose of mortality is eternal, not temporary, and one day our joy will be complete and permanent instead of partial and periodic. We will arrive at our journey's destination to find that however great we thought it would be, it is greater—even beyond anything our mortal minds can comprehend. But because of Christ's infinite sacrifice, we do not have to wait until the hereafter to receive the assurance and healing that atoning grace affords. This is what the Lord promises those who remain steadfast in righteousness:

> For thus saith the Lord—I, the Lord, *am merciful and gracious* unto those who fear me, and delight to honor those who serve me in righteousness and in truth unto the end.
>
> Great shall be their reward and eternal shall be their glory.

And to them will I reveal all mysteries, yea, all the hidden mysteries of my kingdom from days of old, and for ages to come, will I make known unto them the good pleasure of my will concerning all things pertaining to my kingdom.

Yea, even the wonders of eternity shall they know, and things to come will I show them, even the things of many generations.

And their wisdom shall be great, and their understanding reach to heaven; and before them the wisdom of the wise shall perish, and the understanding of the prudent shall come to naught.

For by my Spirit will I enlighten them, and by my power will I make known unto them the secrets of my will—yea, even those things which eye has not seen, nor ear heard, nor yet entered into the heart of man. (D&C 76:5–10, emphasis added)

My hope is that the principles taught in this book will help you lay claim on those blessings. I wish you well as you pursue the permanent state of peace that atoning grace makes possible. May you find much joy in that journey.

WHAT ENOS LEARNED

And I soon go to the place of my rest, which is with my Redeemer; for I know that in him I shall rest. And I rejoice in the day when my mortal shall put on immortality, and shall stand before him; then shall I see his face with pleasure, and he will say unto me: Come unto me, ye blessed, there is a place prepared for you in the mansions of my Father. Amen.
(Enos 1:27)

THIS VERSE SUMMARIZES THE ULTIMATE learning Enos gained from his day in the woods. By acting on truths he had learned since his childhood, he gained an intimate understanding of the Savior's Atonement by *experiencing* it (see Enos 1:1, 3, 5–6). He found out for himself what grace is and the role it could play in his life (see Enos 1:6). He learned what it means to act in faith and have hope fulfilled (see Enos 1:7–8). And he learned that the combination of faith, hope, and grace leads to becoming spiritually complete and whole (see Enos 1:8).

As a result, Enos *was* blessed with an assurance of his place before God. He had come to know Christ and therefore had no fear of the afterlife. To the contrary, he anticipated it with pleasure. He looked forward to greeting his Savior and knew what kind of welcome he would receive when that day arrived. He was granted an assurance of the place he would inherit in the Lord's kingdom. He learned what it means to enter the Lord's rest, both in mortality and in the world to come.

The same can be true for you and me if we will but follow inspired principles and be led by correct doctrine. In short, Enos's story can be our story. We can experience Christ's Atonement as Enos experienced it. We can have our faith rewarded as his was rewarded. We can obtain the same assurance he received. And if we do, in the end, we will know the Savior as Enos knew Him. We, too, will come to know what it means to enter the Lord's rest.

My desire is that this book has succeeded in unlocking this truth for you.

Assessment

To help you determine the extent to which you Allow Christ to Transform You (Principle Five), consider completing this brief assessment. Give each statement a score between 1 and 10 (10 suggesting the statement describes you completely) based on your current state of mind and circumstances.

Your scores will help you identify strengths you can build upon and barriers you need to address as you seek to overcome challenges and make spiritual progress.

1. I understand the meaning of grace.
2. I believe Christ has the power and desire to lighten my burdens.
3. I believe Christ seeks to help me despite my imperfections.
4. I share my burdens with the Lord and ask Him to help me overcome them.
5. I keep the commandments and trust the Lord's grace will be sufficient to help me conquer my trials and weaknesses (see Ether 12:27).
6. I understand and accept this promise from the Lord: "Peace I leave with you, my peace I give unto you: *not as the world giveth, give I unto you.* Let not your heart be troubled, neither let it be afraid" (John 14:27, emphasis added).
7. I have experienced the Lord's tender mercies in my life.
8. I currently recognize and record the Lord's tender mercies as they are manifest.
9. I experience joy in my life and recognize atoning grace as the source of that joy.
10. I believe angels minister to God's children on Earth and can minister to me.

As you review your scores, which areas represent strengths you can build upon? Which are areas that could become potential barriers to your peace if not addressed?

Strengths to Build Upon:
1.
2.
3.

Potential Barriers to Peace:
1.
2.
3.

Consider making notes about the steps you plan to take to improve your application of this principle.

Actions:
    1.
    2.
    3.

EPILOGUE

Lord, how is done?
(Enos 1:7)

HOPEFULLY, THE FIVE PRINCIPLES DISCUSSED in this book have made the answer to Enos's question a little clearer to you. That said, I encourage you to consider what you have learned here as just a starting point in your journey to become spiritually complete. I hope you will view this book as an invitation to pursue an even deeper understanding of the Savior's Atonement and how its power can play a more active role in your life. Part of my intent in writing this book has been to inspire you to engage in that pursuit.

There is so much more to learn about how atoning grace can transform and empower us to achieve our divine potential—certainly more than can be covered in a single work such as this. That is why the Lord has given us five volumes of scripture and modern-day prophets, seers, and revelators to help us learn "line upon line, precept upon precept, here a little and there a little" (2 Nephi 28:30) until we arrive at "the perfect day" (D&C 50:24). It is to the Lord's written word and His leaders we should look for additional guidance and wisdom.

I pray you will persist in your efforts to "come unto Christ, and be perfected in him" (Moroni 10:32). As you do, I can promise you it will not be easy. But I can also assure you that you will not be alone. The Savior Himself will provide the strength you need. Therefore, may the words of this hymn ever offer you encouragement:

> Be still, my soul: The Lord is on thy side;
> With patience bear thy cross of grief or pain.

Leave to thy God to order and provide;
In ev'ry change he faithful will remain.
Be still, my soul: Thy best, thy heav'nly Friend
Thru thorny ways leads to a joyful end.

Be still, my soul: Thy God doth undertake
To guide the future as he has the past.
Thy hope, thy confidence let nothing shake;
All now mysterious shall be bright at last.
Be still, my soul: The waves and winds still know
His voice who ruled them while he dwelt below.

Be still, my soul: The hour is hast'ning on
When we shall be forever with the Lord,
When disappointment, grief, and fear are gone,
Sorrow forgot, love's purest joys restored.
Be still, my soul: When change and tears are past,
All safe and blessed we shall meet at last.
("Be Still My Soul," *Hymns*, no. 124)

Be well.

ACKNOWLEDGMENTS

THE MOTIVATION TO WRITE *LORD, How Is It Done?* grew out of my own experiences with the Atonement of Jesus Christ as well as those I observed or heard about from other members of The Church of Jesus Christ of Latter-day Saints. Once I decided to transform my notes and other writings on the subject into a book, I sought the input and feedback of a few whose opinions and insights I valued. My work was given greater focus and improved because of their involvement. I want to thank and acknowledge them here.

First, I express love and gratitude to my wife, Mattie. Upon learning I was considering this project, she enthusiastically encouraged me to follow through—and has never wavered in that support.

I am grateful to the members of the Tijeras Canyon Ward of the Santa Margarita California Stake, who supported me as their bishop for five-and-a-half years and whose examples and experiences were foundational inspirations for this work. I extend special thanks to those who granted me permission to include their stories in this book.

The stake president during the time I served as bishop was Arlen D. Woffinden. He has been referenced in several chapters. His example and teachings broadened my view of the Savior's Atonement. I am especially grateful for the blessing he gave me when I was ordained and set apart as a bishop—which included special direction and endowments regarding the Atonement. He is an example of the principles you read about in this book, and I have learned much from him over the years.

As I was formulating the structure and direction of *Lord, How Is It Done?*, I solicited the help of two long-time friends who have deep gospel experience and insight. I offer special thanks to Dennis Gladwell and Duane Nichols, whose feedback and perspective early on changed the tone and direction of my writing. Without their input, this book would be less focused. They provided the guiding rudder it needed. Duane passed away before this book was published. I hope there is some way for him to learn how much I appreciate his helpful insights and cherish his friendship. I miss him.

I am also grateful to other individuals who learned of my project during its formation and provided encouragement. One was Kevin Hall, author of *Aspire* (HarperCollins). I met Kevin after being inspired by his book and told him of the writing I was doing. Since my initial breakfast meeting with him, he was consistently encouraging and supportive of my goal to get my own book published.

Other friends and family members took time to read my manuscript and offer feedback before I submitted it to a publisher. Special thanks to Ray Lowry, Valynn Melzer, and Debi Woffinden, whose input was so helpful. Each raised questions, suggested edits, offered challenges, and otherwise made the message of this book clearer and more accessible.

I am grateful for the watchful care and keen oversight provided by my editor at Covenant Communications, Kami Hancock. Her patience gave me relief, and her editing prowess made the book better. Similarly, I am thankful to Robby Nichols, managing director at Covenant Communications, for taking an early interest in my project. He got personally involved to ensure my relationship with Covenant got off the ground smoothly and laid the groundwork for a great partnership. Covenant's Michelle Fryer did amazing design work on *Lord, How Is It Done?*, and Amy Parker, Covenant's marketing director, did a tremendous job ensuring the largest audience possible knew about this book. I am deeply appreciative of their enormous contributions.

My parents are real heroes of mine. I have included accounts from their lives here as well. They are beyond the veil now, but their examples, influence, and love remain guiding forces in my life—and forever will. They provided a home environment in which the principles discussed in this book could take root in me.

Finally, I am grateful to my children and grandchildren, whose love and support also encouraged me during the time I was writing *Lord, How Is It Done?* They frequently asked how my book was coming and expressed confidence in my ability to succeed at what I was attempting. In truth, this book was written for them. To paraphrase Nephi: "For [I] labor diligently to write, to persuade [my] children . . . to believe in Christ, and to be reconciled to God; for [I] know that it is by grace that we are saved, after all we can do" (2 Nephi 25:23).

ABOUT THE AUTHOR

KEN GIBSON IS A HUSBAND, father, and grandfather who has served in a range of leadership positions in and out of The Church of Jesus Christ of Latter-day Saints and remains immersed in his career as a partner in a business-consulting firm. In carrying out his personal, education, career, and Church responsibilities, he has needed to write about complex topics in understandable terms, both in business and in the gospel. This ability ultimately earned him a position as part of BYU's Education Week faculty, for which he teaches concepts he has studied and written about for many years.